THE OLD TRAFFORD EI

ACKNOWLEDGEMENTS

A particular word of thanks should be given to Cliff Butler for his help and encouragement in the compiling of this book. Thanks also to all those at Mainstream Publishing who have been involved with this project, including Bill Campbell, Peter Frances and Janene Reid, and to Stephen Raw for the design of the jacket as well as to the Association of Football Statisticians. Thanks are due also to my agent John Pawsey and gratitude, as ever, to my wife Judith and children Nicholas and Emma.

THE OLD TRAFFORD ENCYCLOPEDIA

An A-Z of Manchester United

Stephen F. Kelly

MAINSTREAM
PUBLISHING

EDINBURGH AND LONDON

For Judith, Nicholas and Emma

First published in Great Britain in 1993 by
MAINSTREAM PUBLISHING COMPANY (EDINBURGH) LTD
7 Albany Street
Edinburgh EH1 3UG

ISBN 1 85158 569 9

A catalogue record for this book is available from the British Library

Typeset in 11/13 Janson by Servis Filmsetting Ltd, Manchester

Printed in Great Britain by the Cromwell Press, Melksham, Wiltshire

A

ABANDONED. United have had many matches abandoned during their history but one of the most bizarre was in March 1909. United were playing Burnley in the quarter finals of the FA Cup and were losing 0–1 with just 18 minutes remaining. United were not playing well and looked all set to be eliminated from the competition. But help was on hand from above. A sudden snowstorm descended on Burnley and amid atrocious conditions the referee was forced to halt proceedings. The game was replayed four days later and this time United won 3–2 and went on to win the FA Cup for the first time in their history.

AGGREGATE SCORE. United's highest ever aggregate score in proper competition came in their first ever tie in Europe, in the preliminary round of the European Cup in 1956. After beating RSC Anderlecht 2–0 in Belgium, United then won 10–0 at Maine Road, to clock up an aggregate score of 12–0. The only other occasion when 12 goals have been scored in a game involving United was in the 1911 Charity Shield when United beat Swindon 8–4.

ALBISTON, ARTHUR. Born in Scotland, Arthur Albiston

came to United as a youngster and went on to make well over 400 appearances for the club. He has the unique distinction of having made his FA Cup debut in a Wembley final when as a 19-year-old he was called up against Liverpool for the 1977 final. Ninety minutes later, after just one Cup game, he was the proud owner of a Cup winners' medal. But the big occasion had never overawed Albiston who had made his senior debut in front of 55,000 as United faced City in a 1974 League Cup game. A strong, thoughtful defender, Albiston took a few seasons to establish himself but by 1978 he was a first team choice and remained a regular until losing his place in 1987. Albiston also won Cup winners' medals in 1983 and 1985 to become the first United player to ever win three FA Cup winners' medals. Capped by Scotland as a schoolboy, he went on to make his full Scottish debut in 1982 against Northern Ireland. By the mid-1980s he had established himself in the heart of the Scottish defence and went on to collect a total of 14 caps, including a trip to Mexico for the 1986 World Cup finals. He played well over 460 games for United. In 1988 he joined West Brom and later had spells with Dundee, Chesterfield and Chester.

AMATEURS. Without question the most prominent amateur to ever play for United was Harold Hardman who won three amateur caps for Great Britain during the 1908 Olympic games as the British side went on to win the gold medal. Hardman also won four full England caps although these were won while he was an Everton player. Other prominent United amateurs have included J. Bradbury, Warren Bradley, M. Pinner and J. Walton who all won England amateur caps while at United.

ANDERSON, VIV. Tall, athletic defender Viv Anderson was signed from Arsenal for £250,000. He was new manager Alex Ferguson's first signing during the summer of 1987. Nottingham-born Anderson kicked off his league career under Brian Clough although he had originally been a

Viv Anderson

trialist at Old Trafford. He went on to become the first black player to ever play for England when he starred against Czechoslovakia in 1979. Anderson had a glittering career at Forest, the winner of two European Cup medals, a league championship medal and two League Cup medals. In 1984 he moved to Arsenal and then a couple of years later, at the age of 31, signed for United. Ferguson bought him for his wealth of experience but it was inevitable that at his age injuries would begin to interrupt his career. He played 37 times during his first season then had just a handful of games the following season. In January 1991 he left Old Trafford and signed for Sheffield Wednesday after playing 64/5 games for United. He was capped 30 times by England, winning just three of his caps while he was a United player. Anderson played in a total of four League Cup finals with Forest and Arsenal.

ANGLO-ITALIAN TOURNAMENT. United competed for this trophy during the 1972–73 season. In their group they faced Fiorentina, Lazio, Bari and Verona. They drew with Fiorentina and Lazio and although they went on to beat Bari and Verona they still failed to qualify for the semi-finals.

APPEARANCES. Bobby Charlton holds the record for the number of appearances for United. In a career that spanned 16 years from 1956 to 1972 he played a total of 752/2 games. Of these, 604 were in the league, 79 in the FA Cup, 24 in the League Cup and 45 in Europe.

ASSISTANT MANAGER. The current assistant manager at United is the former United striker Brain Kidd who succeeded Archie Knox in 1991.

ASTON, JOHN SNR. The strength of United's great post-war side was without question its defence. The combination of Carey and Aston at the back provided a solid foundation from which to build. Yet John Aston began life at Old

Trafford as an inside-forward. He signed for the club as a schoolboy in 1937 but due to the outbreak of war his career never really got going until 1946. But over the next eight seasons he was to prove one of the most reliable defenders in the game, going on to make 282 appearances. He was a member of the 1948 Cup-winning side and the 1952 championship team and collected a total of 17 England caps. He made his England debut in 1949 against Scotland and for the next three years was a regular, partnering Alf Ramsey at the back of what was a generally robust England defence. Aston also made the trip to Brazil for the 1950 World Cup finals where the England defence was embarrassingly caught out on more than one occasion, none more so than in the one-goal defeat by the USA. After that trip Aston played just one more game for England. His greatest strengths were his pace and his passing ability, both perhaps a part of his breeding as an inside-forward. It meant that even though he was a full-back he was always keen to get forward and injuries upfront often allowed him to switch roles, bringing him a total of 30 goals in his Old Trafford career, including 15 league goals during the 1950–51 season as United finished runners up for the fourth time in five seasons. His career ended in 1954, cut short by injury, but it was not to be the end of his days at Old Trafford. Instead he turned to scouting and in 1970 was appointed chief scout. By then his son John was carrying on the family business in the United side. In 1972 the sacking of Frank O'Farrell brought a swift end to his long career at Old Trafford.

ASTON, JOHN JNR. Given his father's long and illustrious career at Old Trafford, it was inevitable that as soon as the young Aston showed some footballing talents he would wind up at United, especially given that his father was also a United scout. He signed for the club as an apprentice and after helping them win the Youth Cup, turned professional in 1964, making his league debut at the end of his first season. By the following year, 1964–65, he was a regular and remained a vital part of United's plans until injury cut short his Old Trafford career. Unlike his father, however, the young Aston was a winger. Calm and uncomplicated, he was the perfect antidote to the unpredictable genius of Best on the other flank. Aston won a championship medal with the 1966–67 side and then went on to play a key role in United's European Cup triumph, even laying on the vital goal for Best in the semi-final against Real Madrid. A modest, unassuming player, Aston's role during United's glorious years has often been underrated. Yet his commitment and endeavour were just as important as the individualistic skills of his colleagues. By the 1971–72 season his appearances were becoming more scarce and a broken leg during that season effectively ended his United career as others stepped into his spot. In July 1972 he was transferred to Luton Town for £30,000 where he enjoyed something of an Indian summer, helping the second division side to win promotion. He later had spells with Mansfield and Blackburn. He played a total of 164/21 games for United, scoring 27 goals.

ATKINSON, RON. Ron Atkinson was United manager between 1981 and 1986. After the dour years of Dave Sexton, United needed a manager with a little sparkle and ambition. Sexton, for all his honest endeavours, had never managed to set the Stretford End alight. Having replaced a larger-than-life character in Tommy Docherty, Sexton then found his thoughtful style cast aside in favour of another flamboyant character. Atkinson, fondly known as Big Ron to the fans, had spent most of his years in the Midlands and in the lower divisions. As a player he had been the driving force behind Oxford United's rise from non-league football to the second division. Then as a manager he guided Cambridge United through the lower reaches towards the second division before West Brom tempted him to the Hawthorns and first division soccer. Success was almost instant and West Brom were soon championship contenders with Atkinson basking in the glory. He was an obvious choice for United. Bold, determined and a good communicator as well as a proven manager, his arrival at Old Trafford initiated a major clear out. Off went Gidman, Thomas and Joe Jordan; in came Stapleton for £1.1 million and then Bryan Robson and Remi Moses from his old club for a combined fee of £2.4 million. But it was to prove money well spent. Later there were other extravagant purchases, including Gordon Strachan, Peter Davenport, Alan Brazil and a couple of foreign imports in Johnny Sivebaek and Jesper Olsen. Not all Atkinson's deals worked – Peter Beardsley slumped off to Canada and Newcastle – but it all brought a touch of excitement to Old Trafford that had been lacking since the cavalier days of Tommy Docherty. Results improved. In his first two seasons in charge Atkinson took United to third place in the league, an FA Cup final triumph over Brighton and a League Cup final appearance against Liverpool. In 1985 they again won the FA Cup and as the 1985–86 season opened it seemed that at last United would clinch the title. Ten consecutive victories left United racing ahead of the pack but they suffered a sudden loss of form and before the autumn was out they had been caught. It seemed that even the spirited Atkinson could not cast the magic spell that would bring the coveted league title back to Old Trafford. The 1986–87 season kicked off to a disastrous start with United losing their three opening fixtures. After nine games they had just one victory. By November they were fourth from bottom and their league hopes had been dashed. Then when they went out of the League Cup, beaten 4–1 by Southampton, Atkinson's Old Trafford career was over. Yet he had survived longer than any post-Busby manager. Atkinson had spent heavily, over £8 million, but had recouped more than £6 million with the sale, among others, of Ray Wilkins and Mark Hughes, though the loss of these two players, perhaps more than anything, tipped the balance against a United title. He had brought some glory to Old Trafford. His spending and champagne style had promised much but in the end had only led to frustration. He was never really popular with the board and the occasional indiscipline of his players off the park only dragged the club's name through the front pages. But Atkinson would never be short of a job. After United he wound up at Sheffield Wednesday and then later at Aston Villa where he found himself challenging United for the league title.

ATTENDANCE – HIGHEST. The highest ever attendance at Old Trafford was for the FA Cup semi-final on 25 March 1939 when 76,962 turned up to watch Wolves beat Grimsby 5–0. The highest ever attendance for a United game was in December 1920 when 70,504 saw United lose 3–1 to Aston Villa in a first division fixture. United's highest post-war attendance at Old Trafford was 66,123 for the first home league match against Nottingham Forest shortly after the Munich disaster. However, a massive crowd of 82,950 watched United play Arsenal in a first division fixture at Maine Road at a time when United were forced to use City's ground due to wartime damage at Old Trafford.

ATTENDANCE – SMALLEST. The lowest ever attendance at Old Trafford was in May 1921 when just 13 people turned up to see a second division fixture between Stockport County and Leicester City. Stockport's ground at Edgeley Park had been closed following crowd disturbances and as County were already doomed to relegation nobody was much interested.

B

BAILEY, GARY. United goalkeeper of the late 1970s and 1980s. The son of Roy Bailey, the former Ipswich Town goalkeeper, Gary spent most of his youth in South Africa where his father was working. Gary was actually playing for Witts University when he was spotted by the one-time United player Eddie Lewis in January 1978. He was subsequently sent to Old Trafford for a trial and by the end of the year had made his first division debut. By the end of his first season he had become the automatic choice and had appeared in a Wembley Cup final. For the next seven seasons Bailey was to be United's first choice keeper, playing in almost 400 games for the club. Bailey was also honoured at full England level, winning two caps and 14 Under-21 caps. In 1983 and 1985 he added FA Cup winners' medals to his collection but a bad knee injury in 1987 brought an end to his United career.

BAMLETT, HERBERT. United manager of the inter-war years. A former referee, Herbert Bamlett had once refereed a cup final, the 1915 game between Burnley and Liverpool. He had also refereed a notorious FA Cup quarter-final between United and Burnley at Turf Moor in 1909 when he abandoned the game with just 18 minutes remaining when United were a goal down and looking certain to be eliminated from the Cup. In the replayed match United won and went on to win the FA Cup. Bamlett took over at Old Trafford in 1927 following the temporary appointment of Clarence Hilditch as player-manager. Bamlett's four years in charge, however, brought little relief, even though he signed the outstanding Tom Reid and Henry Rowley. United were already struggling at the foot of the first division when he took over and when he left at the end of the 1930–31 season they were bottom, having conceded 115 goals. Prior to the United job Bamlett had been in charge of Middlesbrough and had taken them to the top of the second division and to the brink of promotion. He had also managed Oldham and Wigan Borough in his earlier days.

BANK STREET. United's home ground from September 1893 until January 1910, Bank Street, in Clayton, was hardly an attractive ground, standing next to a chemical plant which belched out smoke and fumes for most of a Saturday afternoon, making it most unpleasant for spectators. The pitch was also appalling and most of the time, especially during the winter, it was little better than a mud bath. It was ironic because United had moved to Clayton to get away from the appallingly muddy pitch at North Road. Attendances were generally low at Bank Street even though the move had also been partly inspired by the fact that there was more space for spectators. But for one reason or another they never showed up with most games averaging around 10,000 although as many as 40,000 may have watched the local derbies with City. In 1904 the ground was chosen as the venue for the annual fixture between the Football League and the Scottish League when an estimated crowd of 40,000 turned up. Bank Street's greatest moments came in April 1908 when United beat Preston to clinch their first ever league title. And then, a season later, Bank Street was to see a further triumph when United returned home with the FA Cup. After a tumultuous reception and parade around the streets of Manchester, the team brought the Cup to Clayton where they then faced Woolwich Arsenal in a league fixture. In 1910 the ground was sold to Manchester Corporation for £5,500 and the construction of Old Trafford began. The last ever game played at Bank Street was on 22 January 1910 when United beat Tottenham 5–0 in front of a crowd of just 7,000.

BANKRUPTCY. In 1902 the financial state of Newton Heath reached a perilous low. They owed money left, right and centre, and on 9 January one of their creditors, William Healey, who also happened to be the president of the club, appeared before the County Court in Ashton to initiate a winding-up order. Healey was owed £242, a substantial amount of money in those days, and with the club unable to pay their debt the judge had no option but to declare them bankrupt and begin winding-up proceedings. Although some directors protested, asking for more time, the club was more than £2,600 in debt and no length of time would ever have saved them. The club was in serious trouble and probably came within 24 hours of folding. Although their next game was cancelled as the official receiver moved into Bank Street and closed the ground down, the order at least galvanised support for United, bringing Harry Stafford and eventually John Davies to the rescue with his money.

BARGAIN BUYS. Some of the greatest players in United's history have been among the cheapest. Indeed, Bobby Charlton, George Best, Duncan Edwards, Roger Byrne and Ryan Giggs cost only the official signing-on fee. But where a fee was paid, the bargain of all time was probably Johnny Carey who cost just £250 when he joined United from the Dublin side St James's Gate in November 1936.

BARNES, PETER. Although he is better known as a Manchester City player, Barnes also had a spell at Old Trafford. He came to the club on loan in May 1984 from

Leeds United but returned to Leeds and subsequently joined Coventry. It was then a surprise when United signed him in July 1985. But it never really worked out. Barnes failed to hold on to his place and the club let him rejoin Manchester City in January 1987, the club where he had first made his name. Barnes also had spells with West Bromwich Albion and Real Betis of Seville.

BARNSLEY. Strangely, many of United's players have come to the club via Barnsley. Tommy Taylor, perhaps the greatest centre-forward of his generation came directly from Barnsley, joining United in March 1953 for £29,999. Another great centre-forward who also came from Barnsley was Ernest Hine who played with the club in the early 1930s. An England international, Hine had spells with Leicester and Huddersfield before joining United. Frank Barson, one of the toughest centre-halves of his day was also a product of the Oakwell club, coming to United after spells with them and Aston Villa. Another from Barnsley was George Wall a goalscoring outside left of the Edwardian era who won a championship and an FA Cup medal with United as well as a number of England caps.

BARSON, FRANK. Barson was notorious, said to be one of the toughest centre-halves ever to play for United. He was a Sheffield man who had been a blacksmith before becoming a professional footballer. His career began with Barnsley and then continued at Aston Villa where he won a Cup winners' medal in 1920. He joined United in 1922 for £5,000 with the promise of a public house should United be promoted. United were promoted and Barson was duly given the proprietorship of a pub but there was such a rush when the doors were opened that Barson quickly changed his mind and decided that the life of a publican was not for him. It was odd because Barson was never one to shun a confrontation. In his career he was sent off on numerous occasions and was once rumoured to have threatened the manager of Aston Villa with a gun. Barson was even sent off in his last ever game. All of this may account for the fact that despite Barson's ability as a defender, he was honoured only once by his country, playing for England against Wales at Highbury in 1920. He played 152 games for United over six seasons but was given a free transfer in 1928, and signed for Watford.

BEALE, ROBERT. United goalkeeper in the years immediately prior to the First World War. Beale came to Old Trafford as the club faced a goalkeeping crisis. Their championship goalkeeper Harry Moger had handed over to Hugh Edmonds but with the result that United were conceding goals at an alarming rate. Beale was the man brought in from Norwich City to solve the problem. Although he was a success, his career was effectively ended when war broke out three years later. Beale played 112 games for United.

BEARDSLEY, PETER. The one that got away. It's often forgotten that the England star Beardsley was once a United player. He was signed by Ron Atkinson for £300,000 in August 1982 from Vancouver Whitecaps shortly after he had scored a couple of goals for Vancouver against United in a pre-season friendly. Johnny Giles, the former United player, was managing Vancouver at the time and recommended him to Atkinson. The Newcastle-born Beardsley had begun his career with Carlisle United but although he was being closely watched by a number of clubs nobody was prepared to pay the £300,000 asking price. So instead Beardsley drifted to Canada for a few years. His Old Trafford career seemed to be just as fated as his earlier days in England. He made just one appearance for United, coming on for 45 minutes against Bournemouth in the Milk Cup. In the end he was allowed to rejoin Vancouver but eventually wound up at Newcastle. The rest, as they say, is history. Beardsley then joined Liverpool for £2 million and went on to win most of the honours the game can offer. It was a mistake United would prefer to forget.

BEARDSMORE, RUSSELL. Joined United as a youngster and went on to play more than 60 games for the club. He made his debut during the early part of the 1988–89 season and for a couple of seasons looked to have secured a place in the squad. But the arrival of new players and the keen competition for places saw him struggling as United began their championship season. Although Beardsmore had been at Old Trafford as the trophies began to roll in, he had missed out on most of the big occasions. At the end of the 1992–93 season he joined Bournemouth.

BEHAN, BILLY. United scout for many years, generally regarded as the best the game has ever known. A goalkeeper, he played just once for United, in 1933, before returning to Ireland to take up refereeing and then scouting. During his days as a scout he uncovered some of the finest names in the club's history including Johnny Carey, Johnny Giles, Billy Whelan, Tony Dunne, Don Givens, Ashley Grimes, Kevin Moran and Paul McGrath.

BELL, ALEX. One of the great half-backs of the Edwardian era. Bell was part of a half-back line that consisted of Charlie Roberts, Dick Duckworth and himself. A South African, he was as stylish as they come and enjoyed ten seasons with the club, helping them to two league titles, the FA Cup and second division promotion. In all he played 300 games for United and after the war became a coach with Coventry City and Manchester City. He began his footballing career with Ayr Parkhouse, the Scottish non-league side, and joined United in 1903. He was only 20 years old and cost United £700, a substantial fee in those days. But Bell was well worth it. He was unassuming and modest but highly effective. He was capped once by Scotland in 1912.

BENNION, RAY. Right-half who joined United in April 1920. Bennion went on to play 301 games for the club, winning ten caps for Wales. He left United in November 1932 to join Burnley and retired a few years later.

BENT, GEOFF. United full-back killed in the Munich air disaster who played just 12 league games for the club.

BENTLEY, J. J. United chairman and secretary for many years. Born in 1860, Bentley was one of the founding fathers of football in England. An accountant, he played with Bolton in his early years but gave up playing in 1885 to become secretary of Bolton. Bentley was also a referee and a journalist – he was editor of the great sporting weekly *Athletic News*. He was President of the Football League and in 1902 became chairman of United.

BERRY, JOHNNY. Although Berry is often thought of as a Busby Babe he was in fact 25 years old when he enlisted at United and 31 at the time of the Munich disaster. Berry was signed from Birmingham City after he had given a remarkable display against United at Old Trafford, scoring what is said to have been a 'wonder goal'. He cost United a massive £25,000 but by the end of his first season the club had lifted the league championship. Berry was a typical right-winger. He was just 5ft 5ins but was fast and tricky and ran many a defender ragged with his neat body swerve. In his seven seasons Berry played 273 games for the club, scoring 43 goals. He appeared in the 1957 Cup final and was a member of United's two league championship sides of the mid-1950s. It was also Berry who slammed Tommy Taylor's pass into the back of the net for United's third goal against Athletico Bilbao in their famous 3–0 victory in the European Cup. Berry then played in both games against Real Madrid. By the following season Berry was gradually giving way to others and although he did not play against Red Star he still made the fateful trip to Belgrade. Berry was seriously injured in the Munich disaster and never played football again. But he will always be remembered as a winger whose runs down the right created havoc and gave Taylor and Viollet plenty of opportunities. He was capped four times by England, playing particularly well during the 1953 tour of South America.

BEST, GEORGE. Perhaps the most magical player to ever wear the red of United. Charlton may have been more consistent, Meredith may have been a wizard of dribble and Duncan Edwards may have been a legend, but for sheer excitement nobody could touch George Best. He was in many ways the natural heir to Billy Meredith; enigmatic, equally rebellious and above all an individual. Born in Belfast, he came to Old Trafford as a youngster, got scared and ran back to Ireland with Matt Busby in hot pursuit. Busby was determined not to let him escape. He knew that one day Best would be the man to recapture the passion and challenge of his famous Busby Babes, so tragically killed in Munich. Best made his debut in September 1963, fresh-faced and short-haired. He may have been only 17 but even then he was able to inspire the headlines that dominated the following day's papers. He had made his mark as United beat West Brom and went on to play 26 games that season. Within a year he was the hottest property in soccer. Young, handsome, fashionable, single, and wealthy; he had every-thing. George was a star. He appeared on the front pages and on television. He was spotted in discos and with pretty girls. And on the football field he could tear defences ragged. His twisting, turning and shuffling mesmerised defenders and sent United supporters delirious. He could win a game single-handed. Sometimes he was too much of an individual, often frustrating to play alongside, but then in a moment of magic he would have the ball in the back of the net. His most prolific goalscoring seasons came as United won the European Cup. He scored 32 goals that season and hit more than 20 goals in each of the following four seasons. In the European Cup final he gave one of his greatest displays and was named European Footballer of the Year. He won two championship medals with the club and was undoubtedly one of the greatest names in world football. But he was a restless character. He could never settle, there was always too much going on. Agents, television, the press all exploited him. He turned to drink and when Busby retired in 1969 the one person who had

George Best

kept him in line was gone. Wilf McGuinness tried and failed, so did Frank O'Farrell but by then it was too late. He was disruptive with his genius giving way to self-destruction. He left the club in December 1973 having played 466 games for United with 178 goals. But it was not altogether the end of his career; he later had spells with Hibernian, Fulham, Stockport and in the United States. He later admitted that he had been an alcoholic but overcame the problem and had enough charm to win back his supporters with his perceptive commentaries on radio and TV.

BIRTLES, GARRY. A £1.25 million buy from Nottingham Forest who proved to be something of a disaster at Old Trafford. The highly rated Birtles cost United manager Dave Sexton a record fee in October 1980. Under Brian Clough, Birtles had scored 32 goals in 87 appearances and was at the top of everyone's shopping list. He had also won two European Cup winners' medals, a league championship medal, a League Cup winners' medal and four England caps. But at United he was to prove totally ineffective, scoring just 12 times in 63 outings. In September 1982 United decided to cut their losses and recoup what they could for the young man by selling him back to Forest for £300,000. The failure of Birtles proved costly, not just to United, but also to the man who bought him, Dave Sexton, who was given his marching orders some time before Birtles left.

BLACKMORE, CLAYTON. Another of the many youngsters who have been reared through United's youth ranks. He appeared in the 1982 FA Youth Cup final side and made his debut the following season although he managed only one game. It was the same the season after but in 1985–86 he began to get more opportunities and went on to play more than 200 games for the club. Born in Neath, he won his first Welsh cap against Norway in 1985 and has so far collected more than 30 caps for his country. Blackmore won a European Cup Winners' Cup winners' medal in the 1991 final against Barcelona but was a loser in the 1991 League Cup final against Sheffield Wednesday. He also played in the European Super Cup against Red Star Belgrade.

BLANCHFLOWER, JACKIE. United centre-half whose career was ended through the injuries he sustained at Munich. The brother of Danny Blanchflower, he made his United debut at Liverpool in November 1951. He played just once that season and the following season again made only one appearance but during the 1953–54 season he began to secure his place in the side. He then enjoyed a couple of seasons as a regular choice but after that was generally drafted in as a utility player, filling in for injured colleagues. It meant that in his six seasons playing for United he had only 116 outings but managed a creditable 27 goals in those games. Although he probably enjoyed his best days as a centre-half, Blanchflower could fit in almost anywhere which made him such a valuable player for United. When goalkeeper Ray Wood was injured in the 1957 FA Cup final, it was Blanchflower who pulled on the goalkeeper's jersey to give a brave performance. Blanch-flower made the ill-fated trip to Belgrade for United's European Cup match but did not play against Red Star. In the disaster at Munich he received serious injuries and never played soccer again. He was capped 12 times by Northern Ireland, winning his first cap in 1954.

BONTHRON, ROBERT. Full-back who was unlucky to miss out on United's run of success during the early years of the twentieth century. Scottish-born Bonthron joined United from Dundee in 1903 when United were still a second division side. He was with them for just four seasons, helping United win promotion in 1906. After that he played only one more season with United, however, and consequently missed out as they clinched league and Cup honours over the next few years. Instead, at the end of the 1906–07 season, he joined Sunderland and later had spells with Northampton and Birmingham. In February 1906, playing for United, he was unfortunate to be attacked by the crowd at Bradford after United had thrashed Bradford City 5–1. Bonthron's combative attitude during the game had angered the Bradford supporters and at the end of 90 minutes they invaded the pitch and attacked the United full-back. Arrests followed and a number of spectators were charged with assault.

BOOKS. Among the many books written about Manchester United are the following:

Eamon Dunphy, *A Strange Kind of Glory, Sir Matt Busby and Manchester United*

Geoffrey Green, *There's Only One United*

Stephen F. Kelly, *Backpage United*

Ian Morrison and Alan Shury, *Manchester United, A Complete Record*

David Meek, *Red Devils in Europe*

Tom Tyrrell and David Meek, *Manchester United, The Official History*

BRADLEY, WARREN. One of a number of famous amateur internationals to have played for United, Warren Bradley came to Old Trafford in 1958, just after the Munich disaster. He was already the holder of two amateur Cup winners' medals with Bishop Auckland as well as 11 amateur international caps. He signed professional forms in November 1958 just after making his league debut in the 3–6 defeat by Bolton Wanderers. He went on to play 66 games for United, all on the right wing, and added three full England caps to his collection, the first against Italy in 1959. After four seasons with United he went off to join Bury for £40,000 and later played non-league football.

BRAZIL, ALAN. The former Tottenham and Ipswich player was a surprise signing by Ron Atkinson during the summer of 1984. But despite his well-proven pedigree, Brazil was never quite the outstanding player he had been with

Ipswich. Even at White Hart Lane, he had shown that he was the type of midfielder who could snap up loose chances, yet in his first season at Old Trafford he managed only three goals in 17 appearances. The following season he was just as ineffective. Brazil had cost United £700,000 from Spurs and had been bought to bring some much needed bite to the United midfield. It was hoped that his probing runs might also bring goals as well as make them, but he was to prove a costly disappointment and in the end was sold to Coventry in a deal that brought Terry Gibson to Old Trafford. In all he played just over 40 games for United. Brazil was capped 13 times by Scotland, winning all his caps while he was at Ipswich.

BREEDON, JOHN. United goalkeeper of the inter-war years. Another Barnsley player who found his way to Old Trafford. After beginning his career with Barnsley, Breedon signed for Sheffield Wednesday in 1932 and three years later joined United. His early opportunities were limited by the presence of Irish international Tom Breen, and in his first three years at Old Trafford he had just 13 outings. But at the beginning of the 1938–39 season Breedon finally got his chance, making 22 appearances. He also began the following season as first choice but then war broke out and that was the end of Breedon's career. Just after the war he had a spell as manager of Halifax Town.

BREEN, TOM. Irish international goalkeeper who made 71 appearances for the club between 1936 and 1938, after which he lost his place for John Breedon. Breen began his career with Belfast Celtic before joining United in 1936. He was capped four times while with Belfast Celtic, making his first appearance against England in 1935. He won five caps while at United, his final one in 1939 against Scotland.

BRENNAN, SEAMUS. Popular Irish player who was drafted into the United side in the emergency following the Munich disaster. Brennan, always better known as Shay, had joined the club as a 16-year-old in 1953 but did not get his opportunity until the game immediately after Munich when he gave a mature and inspired performance against Sheffield Wednesday in the FA Cup, scoring twice to give United a 3–0 win. At the time Brennan had been playing as a full-back but came into the side as a winger. He made only a few more appearances that campaign, and the following season played just once. But then in 1959–60 he finally made the break into the first team and was to be ever present over the next ten years, only missing out through injury. In all he played 355 games for the club before quitting in 1970 to join Waterford in the League of Ireland. Brennan was actually born in Manchester of Irish parents but opted to play for the Republic of Ireland, winning 19 caps for his adopted country. Once he was in United's first team he reverted to his old position as a full-back. Brennan's strength was in his tackling. He was never afraid to put a leg in where others might have been more cautious and over the years his assuredness at the back of the United defence gave others the freedom to move upfield without worry. In his years at Old Trafford United won everything and he was just as much a part of that achievement as any of the other, better known, stars. He picked up a European Cup winners' medal and two league championship medals but missed out on an FA Cup medal.

BROTHERS. Among the more famous brothers who have played for United are the Greenhoffs. Brian Greenhoff played for United between 1973 and 1978, while his elder brother Jimmy played between 1976 and 1980. It meant that for a couple of seasons the two brothers lined up regularly for United.

BROWN, JAMES. Glasgow-born wing-half who came to United after playing with East Fife and Burnley. He won a second division championship medal in his first season at the club and was then in the side that was duly relegated at the end of the following season. He was still there when

United were promoted again the season after but was left out of the side as they began the new season in the second division. Brown played 110 games for United, leaving in February 1939 to join Bradford Park Avenue.

BRUCE, STEVE. United captain who became the first United player to lift the championship in 26 years when United won the title in 1993. He began his career with lowly Gillingham where he enjoyed five years of first-team soccer before Norwich snapped him up during the summer of 1984 for £135,000. Bruce was very much the backbone of a useful Norwich side which won promotion and it was hardly surprising that a number of clubs were eyeing up the youngster. But by 1987 his value had also increased and he cost United manager Alex Ferguson £825,000. He went straight into the United side, making a disastrous debut as he conceded a penalty and then broke his nose. But he soon became an automatic choice and has now played over 250 games for the club. He starred in United's FA Cup triumph over Crystal Palace, the League Cup final victory over

Steve Bruce

Nottingham Forest and then the European Cup-Winners' Cup final against Barcelona. A strong, aggressive defender or midfielder who also likes to carry the ball foward, he has scored more than 30 goals for United. Bruce is an inspiring skipper, always setting an example and ready to give everything for the club. Under his guidance United have become a much tougher combination and his impact on United's defence has been crucial.

BRYANT, WILLIAM. Joined United in October 1934 after spells with Wolves and Wrexham. He was an outside-right who could also score goals, and in a United career that stretched to 160 games he netted an impressive 44 goals. Bryant's bad luck was playing in a United side that yo-yoed between the first and second divisions for a number of years. He remained with United when war broke out and continued to play for them throughout the war but when hostilities ceased he opted to join Bradford City.

BUCHAN, MARTIN. Highly popular Scottish defender of the 1970s, recruited by United manager Frank O'Farrell from Aberdeen for £125,000 in March 1972. It was O'Farrell's first major signing and without much question one of his better purchases. Buchan was already a Scottish Footballer of the Year, a Scottish Cup winner and an international by the time he arrived at Old Trafford. He had won his first cap in 1972 against Portugal and went on to win a total of 34 caps over the next seven years, the bulk of them coming while he was a United man. Buchan was a classy defender, strong willed, and an outstanding leader. He had been captain of Aberdeen by the age of 20 and it was not long before he was carrying out a similar task at Old Trafford. Buchan had an immediate effect on a United side lacking confidence and went on to give 12 seasons of loyal service, making 455 appearances. He was captain of the United side that lifted the FA Cup in 1977, making him the first player since the war to captain a Scottish and English Cup winning side. On top of his Cup winners' medals, he also picked up two losers' medals and a second division championship medal. He left United in 1983 to join Oldham Athletic but retired after just one season at Boundary Park. He later had a brief spell as the manager of Burnley. He also had a waspish sense of humour: once asked by a smug TV reporter for a quick word, he replied 'velocity'.

BUCKLEY, FRANK. Major Frank Buckley played only a handful of games for United but was to become one of the finest managers British soccer has ever known. He joined United from Brighton in 1906 but played only three games before moving on to Manchester City in June 1907. At United he came into contact with the club's outstanding manager Ernest Mangnall and no doubt some of Mangnall's wisdom rubbed off on the young man. Buckley played with a variety of other teams before the First World War but then took up management in a glittering career that included Norwich, Blackpool, Wolves, Notts County, Hull, Leeds and Walsall before he retired in 1955.

BURNS, FRANCIS. Another in the long line of United players who came to maturity through the club's junior ranks. Born in Lanarkshire, he had come to Old Trafford as a 15-year-old in 1964. Three years later he was lining up at left-back for the first team as United took on West Ham. He went on to enjoy 45 outings that season, playing in most of the European games but missing out at the end of United's great run through injury. Over the next five years his appearances were generally dictated by his fitness and had injury not been so damaging he would undoubtedly have had many more years and made far more appearances than he did. Ironically, once he left United his injury problem seemed to clear up. He was capped at every level by Scotland but won just one cap as a full international. In June 1972, after 142 games, United sold him to Southampton but with injuries continuing to blight him, he left after a year to join Preston. And it was there that he seemed

Matt Busby

to settle, playing for seven years. He then moved to Ireland, joining Shamrock Rovers.

BUSBY BABES. The name given to the great United team of the mid-1950s because of the many youngsters in the side. The word 'babes' was first used to describe United by *Manchester Evening News* journalist Tom Jackson in November 1951. He used the word as United fielded 18-year-old Jackie Blanchflower and 21-year-old Roger Byrne in a goalless draw at Anfield. As more youngsters came into the side the name stuck and very soon the team generally became known as the 'Busby Babes'.

BUSBY, MATT. Not just the greatest name in the history of Manchester United Football Club but one of the greatest names in the history of soccer. And yet, ironically, Busby's playing days were spent with United's two greatest rivals – Manchester City and Liverpool. Busby was born in Lanarkshire on 26 May 1909 and began his footballing days with Manchester City as a 17-year-old. At the time he was all set to emigrate to the United States with his mother but the City manager persuaded him to come to Maine Road instead. It was a decision that would change the course of his life. He played over 200 league games for City, starring in the 1933 and the 1934 Cup finals, picking up a winners' medal in the latter. He also won his one and only Scottish cap when he played for Scotland against Wales in October 1933. By the mid-1930s City reckoned his days were nearing their end and happily sold him to Liverpool for £8,000. At Anfield his flagging career was suddenly revived when he played in an all-Scottish half-back line alongside Tom Bradshaw and Jimmy McDougall that many rated as the finest in Liverpool's history. It was inevitable that the war would finally spell the end of Busby's footballing career though Busby remained on Liverpool's books until the end of hostilities. He returned to Anfield to be offered a job as assistant manager. But then out of the blue came a letter from Louis Rocca informing him that United were looking for a manager. Within days Busby had met with Walter Crickmer and chairman James Gibson and was duly appointed manager. He was set to become the longest serving manager in United's history. Over the next five years United would be runners-up in the league on four occasions before they finally carried off the title in 1952. They also won the FA Cup in 1948. It was Busby's first great team. A few years later came his second outstanding side, the famous Busby Babes, who lifted two championships before being so cruelly destroyed at Munich. Busby himself was severely injured in the disaster but pulled through and made it to Wembley only to see them lose the FA Cup final to Bolton. At this point anyone else might have been expected to retire but not Busby. He was determined to build another great side and the reconstruction work began immediately. By the mid-1960s he had put together a team that could rival his previous championship sides. And with Best, Law and Charlton they went one step better, winning the coveted European Cup for him in 1968. A year later he decided to retire. Wilf McGuinness took over but it never worked out and in December 1970 Busby stepped in once more until the right successor could be found. He finally quit the manager's chair in June 1971 and was promptly made a director of the club. Under his guidance United had won five championships, the European Cup and two FA Cups. It was an astonishing record. He was awarded the CBE, was knighted after winning the European Cup, was made a Freeman of Manchester in 1967, and has subsequently become President of the club.

BYRNE, ROGER. Few would question the assertion that Roger Byrne was one of the finest full-backs in the history of Manchester United, perhaps even greater than Johnny Carey, and one of the best the English game has ever seen. His death at Munich was a tragedy not just for United but for England as well who might have gone on to win the 1958 World Cup under his inspirational leadership. Born in Manchester, Byrne joined United in 1949 as a 20-year-old

Roger Byrne

but had to wait until he was 22 before making his first-team debut when he played at Anfield against Liverpool. (Jackie Blanchflower also made his debut that day.) Byrne went on to make 24 league appearances that season as United lifted the championship. After that he was a regular in the side, rarely missing a game over the next few seasons. And during that time he skippered United to two more title successes, an FA Cup final and a European Cup semi-final. Byrne was the first of a new breed of full-backs: elegant, fast and a fine distributor of the ball who liked to make runs up the wing. Indeed in his very first season Byrne had played the final six games at outside-left, scoring seven goals that helped United towards the title. But Byrne also had the traditional characteristics of a full-back. He was a tough tackler, uncompromising and committed. He won his first England cap in 1954 against Scotland and went on to win 33 consecutive caps before his death. He made 277 appearances for United, scoring 19 goals.

C

CANADA. United, or Newton Heath, as they then were, played a friendly against Canada in October 1888. The game was played at North Road, Newton Heath winning comfortably.

CANTONA, ERIC. The French striker was a surprise recruit to Old Trafford, joining the club in December 1992 for a little over £1 million. Although Cantona's career had been dogged by incidents and a 'bad boy' reputation, he appeared to have settled at Leeds United where he had won a league championship medal in 1992. But a chance conversation between Alex Ferguson and Leeds manager Howard Wilkinson led to the sensational transfer of Cantona across the Pennines. Since then Cantona has become something of a cult figure among United supporters. Tall, dashing and with a touch of Gallic good looks, he is an explosive player. His skills can be breathtaking and audacious and as long as Cantona is on the pitch no game is ever lost. With Cantona, Giggs and Hughes powering forward, United have begun to adopt a carefree, adventurous approach to their football, reminiscent of the Best, Charlton and Law days of the 1960s. Without much doubt it was the signing of Cantona that gave United an extra dimension leading to their championship success in 1993, making him the first ever player to win championship medals in successive seasons with different clubs. Prior to joining Leeds United, Cantona had played with Nimes, Marseille, Bordeaux, Montpellier and Auxerre in the French league. He has been capped more than 25 times by France.

CANTWELL, NOEL. Irish-born full-back who enjoyed a long and distinguished career with West Ham before joining Manchester United. Born in County Cork, Cantwell signed for West Ham in 1952 when he was 20 and went on to play almost 250 games for the London club. His transfer to United was somewhat unexpected and surprising given that he was already 28 but his experience was to make him a valuable acquisition. He joined the club for £30,000 in November 1960 and went on to captain the side to success in the 1963 FA Cup final. At his age it was inevitable that injuries would disrupt his career and although he spent seven seasons at Old Trafford he managed only 144 appearances. But he was a fine captain, well respected and thoughtful, who, not surprisingly, went on to make an outstanding manager. Many thought he might have become manager of United but when his Old Trafford playing days ended, he went to Coventry. He later had spells at Peterborough and as manager of the Irish national side. He himself had played 36 times for the Republic of Ireland, his first cap coming in 1954 and his final cap 13 years later in 1967.

CAPACITY. The total capacity of Old Trafford in 1993 with the Stretford End seating completed is just over 43,000.

CAPS. The most capped player in United's history is Bobby Charlton with 106 caps for England.

CAPS – ENGLAND. The first United player to be capped by

Eric Cantona

England was Charlie Roberts in 1905. The most capped is Bobby Charlton.

CAPS – IRELAND. The first United player to be capped by

Ireland was M. Hamill in 1912. The most capped Northern Ireland player is Sammy McIlroy with 52 caps and for the Republic Kevin Moran with 38 caps.

CAPS – SCOTLAND. The first United player to be capped by Scotland was Alex Bell in 1912. The most capped is Denis Law with 35 caps during his United career.

CAPS – WALES. The first United players to be capped by Wales were Jack Powell and T. Burke who both appeared against England in February 1887. The most capped Welsh player is Mark Hughes with more than 35 caps.

CAPTAINS. The current United captain is Steve Bruce. Past skippers have included Bryan Robson, Bobby Charlton, Roger Byrne and Johnny Carey.

CAREY, JOHNNY. During the 1940s and early 1950s Manchester United was epitomised by one man – Johnny Carey. There may have been other distinguished players at Old Trafford at the time but Carey stood head and shoulders above all of them. A tall, gentle Irishman off the field, he was a tough, elegant defender on the field. But he was always a gentleman, popular with everyone even those who felt his crunching tackles. Carey was virtually the last player to be signed by manager Scott Duncan. It was ironic because Carey and his other late signing, Jack Rowley, would form the backbone of United over the next dozen years. Carey came to Old Trafford from the Dublin club St James's Gate in November 1936. He had been spotted by the United old hand Louis Rocca who was actually on a spying mission looking at someone else. But as soon as he saw Carey, playing in what was only his third senior game, he signed him immediately for £250. He was to be one of the bargains of all time. It was a full year before Carey found his way into the United first team, making his debut against Southampton in September 1937 at the age of 18. He began as an inside-forward but during the war was converted into a full-back and enjoyed his post-war years in that position, although in his time at United he turned out in just about every position. He was also captain, skippering the side to a famous FA Cup final victory in 1948 against Blackpool and then the league championship in 1952. He was an inspiring captain and it was hardly surprising that when he quit playing he should take up management. He was capped by both Northern Ireland and the Republic of Ireland, winning his first cap in 1937 for Eire against Norway. He won seven caps for Northern Ireland and 29 caps for the Republic, winning his final cap for Eire in 1953. He was captain of Eire the day they beat England at Goodison Park to become the first foreign side ever to win on English soil. He also played for the Rest of Europe against Great Britain in the celebratory international at Hampden Park in 1947. Two years later he was fittingly named Footballer of the Year. In all he played 344 games for United, scoring 18 goals. But for the war, he might well have gone on to break many more records as well as helping United and Eire to even greater achievements. He retired in 1953, spotting that a young full-back named Roger Byrne was ready to take his place. United offered him a coaching position but then Blackburn Rovers came along with an offer to manage their club. Carey later had spells managing Everton, Leyton Orient and Nottingham Forest.

CELTIC. United have never played Celtic in any official competition but they have met in friendlies on a number of occasions, usually for testimonials. Close links have always been maintained between the two clubs who both have strong Catholic traditions. Over the years a number of outstanding players have joined United from Celtic, among them Jimmy Delaney, Pat Crerand, Lou Macari and Brian McClair.

CENTENARY. United's centenary was in 1978. It was celebrated with a friendly match between United and their old rivals Real Madrid at Old Trafford. United won 4–0.

CHAMPIONSHIP. United have won the first division championship on eight occasions: 1907–08; 1910–11; 1951–52; 1955–56; 1956–57; 1964–65; 1966–67; 1992–93.

CHAPMAN, JOHN. Manager of United between 1921 and 1926. Chapman succeeded John Robson as manager of the club but was never able to bring back the glory that United had known prior to the First World War. A Scot, he had been in charge of Airdrieonians for the previous 15 years, turning them into one of the foremost clubs in Scotland. Ironically, one of his final signings for the Scottish club had been the young Hughie Gallacher who would, over the next few years, lead the club to a host of honours. Unfortunately Chapman never seems to have considered bringing Gallacher with him to Old Trafford. Had he done so, he might have enjoyed a more memorable tenure of office. As it was, United just slumped from bad to worse. In his first season they finished bottom of the first division and did not escape the lower division until 1925. Then just as Chapman was beginning to shape his side he was sensationally suspended by the Football Association in October 1926 for alleged 'improper conduct'. United had little option but to sack him. Chapman quietly packed his bags and left Old Trafford and even to this day the reasons for his suspension have never been revealed. Chapman had never really enjoyed much of a footballing career. He had been an amateur with Glasgow Rangers but beyond that had made little or no impact on the game until he became a manager.

CHARITY SHIELD. United have appeared in the Charity Shield on 14 occasions, winning it outright six times and sharing it four times. United also hold the record for the highest score in the competition and the highest aggregate score when they put eight goals past Swindon Town in 1911. A total of 12 goals were scored in that game.

Premier League Champions 1992–93

1908 v Queens Park Rangers (Stamford Bridge) 1–1; replay (Stamford Bridge) 4–0
1911 v Swindon Town (Stamford Bridge) 8–4
1948 v Arsenal (Highbury) 3–4
1952 v Newcastle United (Old Trafford) 4–2
1956 v Manchester City (Maine Road) 1–0
1957 v Aston Villa (Old Trafford) 4–0
1963 v Everton (Goodison Park) 0–4
1965 v Liverpool (Old Trafford) 2–2
1967 v Tottenham Hotspur (Old Trafford) 3–3
1977 v Liverpool (Wembley) 0–0
1983 v Liverpool (Wembley) 2–0
1985 v Everton (Wembley) 0–2
1990 v Liverpool (Wembley) 1–1
1993 v Arsenal (Wembley) 1–1 (5–4 on penalties)

CHARLTON, BOBBY. Wherever the game of football is played the name of Bobby Charlton is up there among the all-time greats. United have had many outstanding players in their history but none surely is as well respected and well known as Charlton. He is the club's top goalscorer and most capped player, and holds the record number of appearances for United. Charlton was born in Ashington, County Durham, the nephew of Jackie Milburn, the former Newcastle and England international. Charlton came to United in the early 1950s and starred in the FA Youth Cup winning sides of 1955 and 1956. In October of 1956 he made his debut against Charlton Athletic and struck two goals. It was a portentous start yet even that was not enough to guarantee him a place in a team of so many talented players. He made just 14 appearances that first season and then the following year began to establish himself in the side as an inside-right. Charlton played in both the home and away legs in United's European Cup quarter-final game against Red Star, scoring twice in Belgrade as United eased themselves into the semi-final. Then came Munich and Charlton crawled from the wreckage to discover that so many of his team-mates, his closest friends, had been killed.

Bobby Charlton

It was an appalling experience yet within days he was back at Old Trafford trying to pick up the pieces. From being one of the babes of the side he was suddenly one of the elder statesmen. He went on to guide United towards a Wembley final and then to help Busby rebuild a side that could win the European Cup. The 1960s were Charlton's years. In the space of just five years he won an FA Cup winners' medal, two league championship medals and a European Cup medal. And as if that was not enough, he also helped England to win the World Cup in 1966. He was the most celebrated player in the country, if not the world. Charlton went on to win a total of 106 caps for England in a period that stretched from 1958 to 1970. His talents were many; he could beat players, pass accurately, head the ball and had a wicked shot. In 754 games for United he scored 247 goals. He was awarded the OBE, and elected European Footballer of the Year in 1969 as well as Footballer of the Year in 1965–66. He finally retired in 1974 and became manager of Preston. But it was not a very successful career as Preston slid into the third division. He later had a brief spell managing Wigan but despite all his playing talents he never really took to the managerial game, unlike his brother Jack. Old Trafford was where he belonged and fortunately there were enough people at the club to realise that he still had much to offer and he was made a director, an honour he well deserved.

CHILTON, ALLENBY. One of the outstanding members of United's post-war championship and Cup-winning side. Chilton joined the club from Seaham Colliery shortly before the outbreak of war and made his debut for United on 2 September 1939 against Charlton Athletic. The following day war was declared and league football went into hibernation for seven long years. During this time Chilton guested for various clubs including Charlton where he won a Southern Cup winners' medal. After the war he had to begin all over again. What's more he was 28 years of age and had been wounded in the Normandy landings. Yet in his first season he managed 43 appearances and in the nine seasons following the war played almost 400 games. With Chilton in the number five shirt at centre-half, United were always composed at the back. There was little that ruffled the big man. He was a member of United's Cup winning side of 1948 and of the league championship team of 1952. He also succeeded Johnny Carey as skipper and picked up two England caps, his first in 1951. In March 1955, after 17 years at Old Trafford, he took over as player-manager at Grimsby Town, taking them to the third division-north championship within a year. He remained there until 1960 when he became manager at Wigan Athletic.

CHISNALL, PHIL. One of the few players in post-war football to have been transferred between Manchester United and Liverpool. Chisnall, an England schoolboy star, joined United from his Manchester school in 1958. He played 47 games for United and had scored 10 goals when Bill Shankly signed him in April 1964 for £25,000. But it never worked out for him at Anfield and after just six league appearances Chisnall was sold three years later to Southend for £12,000.

CLIFF, THE. United's training ground in Lower Broughton, Salford. It was at one time the home of Broughton Rangers, the rugby league club.

COACHES. Current members of the United coaching staff include Brian Kidd, who is assistant manager, Jim Ryan, Nobby Stiles, Eric Harrison, who looks after the youngsters, David Ryan who is the football community officer, Bryan Robson, Jimmy Curran, Joe Brown and Paul McGuinness.

COCA-COLA CUP. See Football League Cup.

COCKBURN, HENRY. Cockburn was another member of United's fine post-war side who gave many years' loyal service to the club. He came to Old Trafford in 1944 and made his league debut as football resumed with the 1946–47 season. Between then and 1954 he played more than 270 games for the club. It was not long before he received international recognition, winning his first cap in 1947 against Wales. His thirteenth and final cap came five years later in 1952 as he lined up for England against France. Although he was on the short side, just 5ft 4ins, Cockburn was a determined wing-half. He could tackle, run like a demon and pass the ball with uncanny accuracy. He brought a touch of elegance to the United half-back line, and for that matter to the England midfield as well. He was a member of United's Cup-winning side of 1948 and was ever present during the championship season. In fact, in his nine years at Old Trafford, Cockburn missed only a handful of games for the club, at one stage going 166 consecutive games. In 1954 he left United to join Bury and later had spells with Peterborough and various other non-league sides. In February 1961 he was appointed assistant trainer at Oldham and then became a coach at Huddersfield Town.

COLMAN, EDDIE. Busby Babe killed in the Munich disaster. Like so many of the United players at that time Colman was a product of United's youth teams, appearing in three FA Youth Cup winning sides. He turned professional in November 1953 on his seventeenth birthday and made his debut during the championship season of 1955–56, playing 25 league games and picking up a champions' medal. He could hardly have made a better start to a career and yet he was still only 19 years old. He won a second championship medal the following season, missing only a few games and also lined up for United in the Wembley Cup final which they lost to Aston Villa. Colman was the natural successor to Henry Cockburn: he was much the same size, took up similar positions and had the same kind of energy, enthusiasm and determination to get forward. He was very much the modern kind of midfielder. He also had a body swerve that soon became a hallmark of his style. Although he was never capped by England there can be little doubt that his name had been pencilled in for the future and that he would have gone on to make many appearances for his country. As it was, he was to die, still only 21 years old, and with so much to contribute. He had played just 107 games for the club.

COLOURS. Over the years United have played in a variety of colours although red has always been the most prominent colour of all. They began life, however, playing in green with gold shorts. Then in 1896, they changed to white shirts with blue shorts. Between 1902 and 1926 they wore red shirts and white shorts. For four years between 1923 and 1927 they sported white shirts with red and white shorts. At times during the early 1930s they also wore white shirts with cherry hoops and white shorts but in 1934 they reverted to wearing their famous red shirts and white shorts. Team photos during the 1913–14 season also show them playing in red and white vertical stripes. Nowadays United's colours only change when they are forced to wear their second strip.

CONNELLY, JOHN. Arrived at Old Trafford already clutching a championship medal, won with Burnley in 1960, as well as a Cup losers' medal and ten England caps. Connelly had come to Old Trafford in search of more honours and he would not be disappointed. He joined the club from Burnley in April 1964 and made his debut as the new season kicked off. By the end of the campaign he had added another championship medal to his collection and a few more England caps. He remained with United for just over two seasons, playing 113 games and scoring 35 goals. A strong, forceful winger he was very much a part of Alf Ramsey's plans until the England manager eventually decided against wingers. He was a member of the England World Cup winning squad, playing in the opening game against Uruguay. Unfortunately it was also to be the last of his 20 games for England.

COPPELL, STEVE. Long-time favourite of the Stretford End and later a highly successful manager. Born in Liverpool, Steve Coppell came to Old Trafford from Tranmere Rovers, recommended to Tommy Docherty by Bill Shankly. Shankly, then acting as a consultant to the Wirral club, was said to have repeatedly told the Anfield board about Coppell but when they failed to show any interest he angrily passed on the information to his old pal Tommy Docherty. Liverpool's loss was to be United's gain. That was in March 1975. Coppell, who was a university graduate, cost just £40,000 and was to go on to play almost 400 games, scoring 70 goals for the club, and to pick up 42 England caps. Coppell was a fast winger with the ability to cut inside as well as to race down the flanks. He would have played many more games for United and possibly won more England caps had his career not been so cruelly cut short by injury. As it was he won a Cup winners' medal in 1977 against Liverpool, and a couple of losers' medals as well. Injury, however, kept him out of the 1983 Cup winning side. He won his first England cap in November 1977 against Italy in the World Cup qualifiers and was a member of the 1982 World Cup squad that went to Spain. He played his last match for England in 1983 against Greece. By then a persistent knee injury was interrupting his appearances. He finally gave up the battle against injury in the summer of 1983 and accepted the offer of a job as manager of Crystal Palace. At 28 he was to be the youngest manager in the Football League. He resigned the post during the summer of 1993, following Palace's relegation.

CRERAND, PAT. Although Crerand was born in Scotland and came to Old Trafford from Celtic he has remained loyal to United and is still to be heard as an articulate commentator on club affairs. Crerand was as tough as they come, perhaps a mark of the fact that he was born in the Gorbals where footballers are said to be forged from iron. Coming from an Irish Catholic background, it was little wonder that he began his footballing career with Celtic. At that time Celtic were still a sleeping giant and Crerand opted for a chance south of the border with United, joining the club in February 1963 for £56,000. Had he stayed, he might well have become a member of Celtic's famous European Cup winning side. As it was, he had a glittering career as part of United's European Cup winning team. He was to play nearly 400 games for the club. Crerand was the muscle in United's half-back line, the player who was not afraid to tackle and win balls. And once he had won the ball he could distribute it as accurately and over as long a distance as anyone in the Football League. He was a dream to watch, the kind of player every successful side needs. What's more, he was popular with players and fans alike who all seemed to appreciate the valuable role he played. He was capped 16 times by Scotland in a five-year period from 1961, with five of those caps coming while he was with United. At the end of the 1970–71 season he joined United's coaching staff, later becoming assistant manager. In 1976 he was appointed manager of Northampton Town but soon returned to his adopted home of Manchester to run a public house.

CRICKET. Being so close to Old Trafford cricket ground it is hardly surprising that one or two United players have also excelled at cricket. One of the most prominent was Freddie Goodwin who made over 100 appearances for United during the 1950s and also played for Lancashire County Cricket Club where he made 11 appearances, scoring only 47 runs but taking 27 wickets. Perhaps a more unexpected footballing cricketer was Noel Cantwell who represented the Republic of Ireland not only at soccer but also at cricket.

CRICKMER, WALTER. United secretary for many years. Crickmer was appointed secretary of United in 1926 and continued in that role until his death in the Munich air disaster in February 1958. During his many years as secretary he also had two spells of managing the club though this amounted to little more than team selection. He took over as manager after the sacking of Herbert Bamlett at the end of the 1930–31 season. It was meant to be a temporary arrangement with United expecting to appoint a new manager by the beginning of the new season. Instead Bamlett found himself having to act as manager with the help of scout Louis Rocca until July 1932 when Scott Duncan was eventually given the job. During the whole time Crickmer continued with his duties as club secretary but was again forced to take over as manager in 1937 when Scott Duncan resigned. No immediate appointment was made and Crickmer once again came to the rescue. Then came war, with no real need for a managerial appointment. After the war Crickmer was responsible for appointing the Liverpool player Matt Busby as manager. Crickmer was also said to have played a large part in the setting up of Busby's youth policy.

CROMPTON, JACK. Goalkeeper in United's post-war Cup winning side. Crompton was a local boy who joined United in 1944. He made his league debut against Grimsby as the 1946–47 season got underway and for the next few seasons was automatic choice. He played in the Wembley Cup final against Blackpool, bringing off a spectacular save close to the end of the game that kept Blackpool at bay. A couple of seasons later, however, he lost his place to Reg Allen but battled back to regain the keeper's jersey during the 1952–53 season. But it was only for a short spell. By then United had signed Ray Wood and after 1953 Crompton's opportunities were limited. He quit United in 1956 to become trainer at Luton Town but returned to Old Trafford following the Munich disaster to help Jimmy Murphy. He played 211 games for the club.

CROWTHER, STAN. One of United's first signings in the emergency following the Munich air disaster. Crowther was signed from Aston Villa, just 75 minutes before United were due to face Sheffield Wednesday in the fifth round of the FA Cup. Although Crowther was actually cup-tied, the FA agreed to waive the rule and Crowther pulled on a United shirt to make his debut in one of the most emotional matches ever played at Old Trafford. Ironically, Crowther had played for Aston Villa against United in the previous year's Cup final and as United stormed to a second successive final Crowther found himself playing at Wembley again, this time for a different side. Although he was still only 22, Crowther came into a United side that made him look like a veteran. He was a skilful young player with 50 games to his credit at Villa and an England Under-23 cap. Yet his United career did not last very long. He made just 18 appearances that season, including the Wembley Cup final and before the year was out had signed for Chelsea. He did not last much longer there either, playing only 51 games before joining Brighton where he managed only four matches. After that he retired even though he was still only 25 years of age. It was a career that had promised so much but in the end had mysteriously petered out.

CURRY, TOM. United trainer of the 1950s who was killed in the air disaster at Munich.

D

DALY, GERRY. Irishman Gerry Daly was signed by Tommy Docherty in April 1973 from the Irish club Bohemians for just £20,000. He was only 19 years old when he joined United but was soon part of an exciting midfield that swept to the second division title in front of record gates. Daly also played in the 1976 Cup final when United lost to Southampton. Unfortunately his United career came to an abrupt end after a row with manager Tommy Docherty and he was transferred to Derby County for £175,000 in March 1977. He had played 137 games for United, scoring a useful 32 goals. Later he had spells with Coventry, Birmingham and Shrewsbury. Daly was capped 47 times by the Republic of Ireland.

DAVENPORT, PETER. Birkenhead-born striker who starred with Nottingham Forest before United bought him for £500,000 in 1985. At Forest Davenport was finding the net every other game and just about every club in the first division was coveting the young man's talents. He had even won himself an England cap and looked set for a glorious career. United manager Ron Atkinson won the race for his signature against hot competition and much was expected

Peter Davenport

of the young man but once he was ensconced at Old Trafford the goals suddenly dried up. He managed just 22 in his 92 games for United. When new manager Alex Ferguson arrived he gave Davenport a vote of confidence but the goals still failed to materialise and in 1988 Ferguson sold him to Middlesbrough. But even with another club Davenport still failed to reproduce the style and goals that had made him such an exciting prospect at Forest. At Ayresome Park his record was even more dismal – seven goals in 59 games – and he was soon on his way to Sunderland. Perhaps the temperament and style of Brian Clough were more atune to his career.

DAVIES, JOHN. The saviour of United in 1902 when his money saved the club from certain extinction. Davies also gave the club a £60,000 grant in 1910 to help build its new stadium at Old Trafford. He also served as chairman for many years.

DAVIES, WYN. Striker signed by manager Frank O'Farrell from Manchester City in 1972. Davies was already a big name when United signed him, having starred with Wrexham, Bolton Wanderers and Newcastle United. But at

John Davies

Old Trafford he was never a success and managed just 16 appearances and four goals. The arrival of Tommy Docherty spelt the end of his days and in June 1973 he was sold to Blackpool. He later had spells with Crystal Palace, Stockport and Crewe. He was capped three times while at Old Trafford but won a total of 34 Welsh caps.

DAWSON, ALEX. Busby Babe who missed the trip to Belgrade. Dawson signed professional forms for United in May 1957 when he was just 17 years old, having already featured in the Youth side. He was a member of the FA Youth Cup winning sides of 1955–56 and 1956–57. He was given his first opportunity shortly before he signed professional forms, making his debut in the 2–0 win over Burnley at Old Trafford as he replaced the unavailable Tommy Taylor. United had already won the title with three games remaining. Yet it was to be a remarkable start to Dawson's career as he scored on his debut. He was then chosen for the next two games, the final two of the season, and scored in both. Three games and three goals. With Taylor fit again, however, Dawson's chances were always going to be limited and he saw action only once more before the Munich disaster. On that occasion United were beaten 0–3 by Portsmouth at Old Trafford. After the Munich disaster Dawson became a regular, ending the season with a creditable five league goals in 12 outings. He also scored in the famous Cup victory over Sheffield Wednesday and hit a hat-trick in the 5–3 semi-final win over Fulham to give him a season's total of ten goals in 18 matches. Dawson's best season for the club, however, was in 1960–61 when he notched up 20 goals in 34 games. But then David Herd arrived and his right to the number nine shirt was gone. He was eventually transferred to Preston North End in October 1961 for £18,000. He had played 93 games for United, scoring an impressive 54 goals. He played in Preston's FA Cup losing side of 1964 and later had spells with Bury, Brighton and Brentford.

DELANEY, JIMMY. Star of United's post-war team. Born in Scotland, Delaney began his footballing days with Celtic, winning a Cup winners' medal in 1937 and nine Scottish caps. He joined United just after the war and was soon on his way to winning another Cup medal, this time as United beat Blackpool in the FA Cup. Delaney later added a league championship medal to his collection and a few more Scottish caps. A tricky little winger with a useful turn of speed, he went on to play 183 games for United, scoring 28 goals over five seasons. He finally left United in 1950, returning to Scotland to join Aberdeen. He later played with Falkirk and Derry City where he played in an Irish Cup winning side to give him a unique trio of Cup winners' medals.

DEFEAT – WORST. United's worst defeat was in the first division in April 1926 when they lost 0–7 to Blackburn Rovers. In December 1930 Aston Villa beat them by the same margin at Villa Park, again in a first division fixture,

THE OLD TRAFFORD ENCYCLOPEDIA

and almost precisely a year later Wolves won 7–0 at Molineux, this time in a second division game.

DEFEATS – FEWEST. During the 1905–06 season United lost just four games in 38 matches in the second division. They lost once at home and finished second.

DEFEATS – MOST. United's worst ever season was 1930–31 when they lost 27 games. Nine were lost at home and a staggering 18 were lost away.

DEFEATS – SUCCESSIVE. United's worst ever run in league football was in 1930 when they lost 14 successive league games, including the first 12 of the 1930–31 season.

DEFENSIVE RECORDS – BEST. United's best ever season was 1924–25 when they conceded just 23 goals as they finished second in the second division.

DEFENSIVE RECORD – WORST. United's worst ever defensive record was the 1930–31 season when they conceded 115 goals to finish bottom of the first division.

DERBY MATCHES. The first ever league derby match against Manchester City was played in front of 15,000 spectators on Saturday 3 November 1894 at Ardwick. United, then known as Newton Heath, won 5–2.

DOCHERTY, TOMMY. The swashbuckling Tommy Docherty became manager of Manchester United in December 1972. He was a replacement to the dour, drab approach of Frank O'Farrell. Docherty was seen as the kind of man who would bring a return to the exciting, adventurous football that had marked the Busby years. Docherty seemed to be the perfect choice. He had already proved himself in a managerial career that had hit the heights at Chelsea and then taken him to Aston Villa, Queens Park Rangers,

Rotherham and Oporto. And before his career was over he would have added another half dozen clubs to his CV. As a player, Docherty had been a tough, combative wing-half with Preston North End, Arsenal and Chelsea, picking up 25 Scottish international caps en route. He was energetic, a players' man, forthright and personable enough to quickly set up a rapport with the Stretford Enders. He took over with United in serious trouble and managed to steer them clear of relegation but it was only putting off the inevitable: the following season they plunged into the second division. But they were soon back as Docherty's young side began to mature into one of the most talked-about and exciting teams in English football. Prior to his appointment, Docherty had been in charge of the Scottish squad where he had seen at close hand all the new potential talent north of the border. It was hardly surprising that some of it found its way to Old Trafford. He brought in players like George Graham, Lou Macari, Jim Holton, Stewart Houston, Alex Forsyth and Jim McCalliog, as well as Englishmen Steve Coppell, Gordon Hill and Stuart Pearson. It was an impressive and costly line-up. But it worked. In their first season back in the first division they finished in third place and reached the FA Cup final, losing to Southampton. The following season they won the Cup, beating league champions Liverpool to rob them of the double. Everything seemed to be going so well. And then the news broke. Docherty had been having an affair with the wife of the club's physiotherapist. The story was splashed all over the front pages. United were in a difficult position. It was proving extremely embarrassing for a club with a strong Catholic tradition and in the end Docherty was asked to leave. It was probably true that Docherty's style of management suited the Stretford Enders more than the directors. Docherty was his own man and in the end his carefree attitude was probably his undoing. Nevertheless, his short reign at Old Trafford is still fondly remembered by many as one of the most exciting of recent years.

DONAGHY, MAL. Northern Ireland international who made his United debut in 1988. He also won his first cap that year and went on to make more than 100 appearances for United before manager Alex Ferguson decided to dispense with his services.

Mal Donaghy

DOUBLE. Although United have never achieved the coveted league and FA Cup double they have come close on a number of occasions. In 1957 they won the league title but were then defeated at Wembley by Aston Villa in the FA Cup final. And in 1948, while finishing second in the league, they went on to lift the FA Cup. The only season when United have won more than one trophy was in 1991 when they won the European Cup-Winners' Cup, the European Super Cup and came within a whisker of winning the League Cup but went down 0–1 at Wembley to

THE OLD TRAFFORD ENCYCLOPEDIA

Sheffield Wednesday.

DOWNIE, ALEX. Edwardian half-back who just missed out on United's glorious era. Born in Scotland, Downie played his early football with Third Lanark before joining Bristol City and then Swindon Town. In 1902 he signed for United, even scoring on his debut. He played regularly in the side that was promoted from the second division in 1906 but enjoyed only ten matches a few seasons later as United clinched the league title. He also missed out on United's Cup final victory over his former club, Bristol City. In 1910, after 191 games and 14 goals, he moved to Oldham Athletic and later ended his career with Crewe Alexandra.

DOWNIE, JOHN. Another famed name from United's outstanding post-war side. Downie was signed from Bradford Park Avenue in 1949 for a club record fee of £18,000. He had an enormous responsibility when he joined the club since he had been bought as a replacement for the popular but troublesome Johnny Morris who had been in dispute with manager Busby. Downie, however, carried out his responsibility with enthusiasm and skill and soon became as popular as his predecessor. He was a Scotsman, born in Falkirk, who had signed for Bradford at the end of the Second World War. Downie went on to play five seasons with United for whom he made 115 appearances, scoring 36 goals, and picked up a league championship medal in 1952. Downie eventually lost his place during the 1952–53 season and opted to join Luton Town in a £10,000 deal. He later played with Hull City, Mansfield Town and Darlington.

DUBLIN, DION. Young striker signed from Cambridge United for £1 million in 1992. At Cambridge he had scored 52 goals in 156 league outings. Unfortunately he broke his leg after just three games with United and spent the rest of the season watching from the stands. Nevertheless, much is expected of him in future seasons with his goalscoring instinct likely to be put to good use in the years ahead.

DUCKWORTH, DICK. One of the great half-backs of the Edwardian era. A local lad, he joined United at the turn of the century and made his debut in December 1903, scoring in the 4–2 win over Gainsborough. But it was to be a couple of seasons before Duckworth fully established himself. He played just ten games in United's second division promotion seasons but after that became an ever present, winning two league championship medals and an FA Cup winners' medal with the club. He was a strong, committed, inspirational player in an outstanding half-back line alongside Charlie Roberts and Alex Bell. He went on to play 251 games for United, scoring 11 goals, and was with the club until the outbreak of war. Yet despite United's success and Duckworth's huge contribution, he was never awarded a full England cap, his only honour coming when he played in a Commonwealth international during the 1901 tour of South Africa. He did, however, play for the Football League on five occasions.

DUNCAN, SCOTT. United manager 1932–37. A former outstanding player, Scott Duncan became United manager in 1932 after Walter Crickmer had been temporarily in charge of the team. In his footballing days Duncan had played with Dumbarton, Glasgow Rangers and Newcastle and also had the distinction of being one of the few players to have ever played with Rangers and Celtic when he played a couple of friendlies with Celtic during the First World War. He had also played one game for United during the First World War. Before taking over at United he had been the manager of Cowdenbeath for five years. Sporting his ever-present trilby, he soon settled into his new post and although he was to become one of United's longest-serving managers he had only mixed fortunes. They were not good years for the club. United were in serious financial difficulties again and spent much of Scott Duncan's reign in the second division, almost plummeting into the third division at one stage. But they were finally promoted in 1936 only to crash back into the lower division the following season. That marked the end of Scott Duncan although at least his lasting legacy to the club was the signing of two players who would eventually bring some pride back to Old Trafford – Johnny Carey and Jack Rowley. A few days after his resignation in November 1937 United beat Chesterfield 7–1 and began a run that would carry them to promotion. Duncan instead became manager at Ipswich Town, taking them into the Football League. In the end he had promised much for Manchester United but had failed to deliver.

DUNNE, TONY. The ever-popular Tony Dunne played just over 500 games for United between 1960 and 1973. He was a full-back, a fine distributor of the ball and a defender who liked to play himself out of trouble rather than opt for the kick into touch. Born in Dublin, he came to Old Trafford in August 1960 from the League of Ireland club Shelbourne United. He had just three outings in his first season but by the following season had secured his place which he was to hold for the next 12 years. He played in the 1963 Cup final and starred in United's championship winning side of 1965 and 1967 before inspiring United to their European Cup triumph over Benfica with a memorable performance at the heart of the United defence. He won his first Irish cap at the age of 20 and went on to collect a total of 33 caps, 24 of these while he was with United. He finally quit United in 1973 and signed for Bolton Wanderers where he continued to give yet more loyal service before he joined the exodus to the United States.

DUXBURY, MIKE. Duxbury served his apprenticeship at Old Trafford, turning professional in 1976 but had to wait until 1980 before making his league debut. But once he was in the side he was there to stay. His early career was as a utility player, fitting in wherever necessary but eventually he settled into the right-back spot and went on to impress at all levels, even winning ten England caps. He won a couple of FA Cup winners' medals with the side, featuring in the 1983 and 1985 FA Cup final victories and also played in the losing 1983 League Cup final match against Liverpool. He won his first full England cap in 1983 against Luxembourg after having won seven caps at Under-21 level. He eventually lost his right-back spot when United signed John Gidman from Everton but Duxbury was still versatile enough to keep his place in the side in various other positions. In all he played well over 300 games for United but left the club at the end of the 1989–90 season when he was given a free transfer and joined Blackburn Rovers.

E

EDWARDS, DUNCAN. Those who saw Duncan Edwards play, and he made just 175 appearances for United, swear that he was the finest half-back of all time, let alone the finest to ever play for United. Had Edwards lived, he would undoubtedly have gone on to become one of the most honoured players in the game. He would have been only 29 in 1966 when England won the World Cup and who knows what other trophies United might have lifted with Edwards pulling the strings in midfield or defence. He was a giant of a player who showed a maturity years beyond his age. At 16 he was 5ft 10½ins tall and weighed 12 stone 6lbs. When he died he had already won 18 full England caps. His first cap had come in 1955 when he was only 18 years and 183 days old, the youngest ever England player. That day England beat Scotland 7–2. He was also capped six times at Under-23 level, played four times for the Football League and once for England B. Edwards had signed for United just hours into his sixteenth year. So convinced was Busby that the youngster had the makings of an outstanding player that he even travelled to his home in the Midlands to secure the lad's signature. Busby was taking no chances. Edwards made his first appearance in April 1953 aged 16, against

Duncan Edwards

Cardiff City, one of the youngest-ever United players, and although United lost 1–4 Edwards showed enough potential to secure his place in the team the following season. From then on he was an automatic choice. Over the next few seasons he went on to win two championship medals and an FA Cup losers' medal. He was the complete player: tall, powerful, strong and fast. His passing was accurate and inventive, his defending sure and simple. He could even score goals, netting 21 in his short United career and five for England. But of course tragedy struck at Munich and the man who would almost certainly have captained England and United to even greater successes was struck down when he was still only 21 years old.

EDWARDS, LOUIS. Director and chairman of United. Louis Edwards became a director of United in 1958, having been introduced to United circles by Matt Busby. By 1965 he had become chairman and principal shareholder and although he was to be highly criticized, not least by a *World in Action* investigation into his financial affairs, it was Edwards who was largely responsible for turning Old Trafford into a super stadium as well as backing Busby in some of his more expensive transfer deals. He died in 1980 shortly after the revelations in the Granada TV programme.

EDWARDS, MARTIN. The current United chairman and chief executive. He became chairman after the death of his father, Louis Edwards, in 1980. He presided over the public flotation of United and, although he was clearly tempted to sell the club some time later, he changed his mind and has continued to give United unstinting support and commitment ever since.

EUROPEAN CUP. United have competed in the European Cup five times. They first participated, much against the wishes of the FA and Football League, at the start of the 1956–57 season. Their first match was against Anderlecht in Belgium on 12 September 1956. That season they went on to reach the semi-finals where they lost to Real Madrid. They competed again the following year, once more reaching the semi-finals, but lost to AC Milan. Their next

appearance came in 1965–66 where they again reached the last four only to lose to Partizan Belgrade. At their next attempt, 1967–68, United went on to win the trophy, beating Benfica 4–1 in extra time at Wembley. The following year they reached the semi-finals yet again, this time losing to AC Milan. In all five of their appearances in the tournament United have reached the last four.

EUROPEAN CUP-WINNERS' CUP. United have competed in the European Cup-Winners' Cup on five occasions, winning the trophy in 1991. Their first appearance was in September 1963 against Willem II Tilburg. That season they went on to reach the quarter-finals, eventually losing to Sporting Lisbon. They next appeared in the competition in 1977–78 when they reached the second round only to be defeated yet again by a Portuguese club. In 1983–84 they participated for the third time and on this occasion reached the semi-finals where they lost to Juventus. United finally made the breakthrough to the final during the 1990–91 season where they met Barcelona in the final in Rotterdam, winning 2–1. As holders of the trophy, United automatically participated in 1991–92 but lost to a fine Atletico Madrid side in the second round.

EUROPEAN FOOTBALLER OF THE YEAR. Three United players have won the coveted title European Footballer of the Year awarded by the French magazine *France Football*:
1964 Denis Law
1966 Bobby Charlton
1968 George Best

EUROPEAN SUPER CUP. United have appeared in this tournament on just one occasion, in 1991, when they defeated the European Cup holders Red Star Belgrade 1–0 in a one-off game at Old Trafford.

F

FA CUP. United first participated in the FA Cup in 1886 when they were drawn away to Fleetwood Rangers in the first round. After 90 minutes the score stood at 2–2 but United, then known as Newton Heath, refused to play extra time and the tie was awarded to Fleetwood.

FA CUP FINAL. The final has been played three times at Old Trafford. It was first played there in 1911 after Bradford City and Newcastle had drawn their first game. The replay at Old Trafford was watched by 56,000 people, with Bradford winning 1–0. The final was next played there in 1915 when just under 50,000 saw Sheffield United beat Chelsea. Old Trafford was chosen as the venue because the Crystal Palace had been turned into a military camp. The 1915 final became known as the Khaki final because so many soldiers in uniform were among the crowd. The third final was also a replay, played in 1970, when Chelsea beat Leeds United. It was the first time a Wembley final had ever been replayed and was seen by 62,000 spectators.

FA CUP FINALS. United have appeared in 11 FA Cup finals, winning the trophy on seven occasions.

1909 v Bristol City (the Crystal Palace) 1–0
1948 v Blackpool (Wembley) 4–2
1957 v Aston Villa (Wembley) 1–2
1958 v Bolton Wanderers (Wembley) 0–2
1963 v Leicester City (Wembley) 3–1
1976 v Southampton (Wembley) 0–1
1977 v Liverpool (Wembley) 2–1
1979 v Arsenal (Wembley) 2–3
1983 v Brighton (Wembley) 2–2 (*aet*)
Replay (Wembley) 4–0
1985 v Everton (Wembley) 1–0
1990 v Crystal Palace (Wembley) 3–3 (*aet*)
Replay (Wembley) 1-0

FA CUP SEMI-FINALS. United have reached the semi-finals of the FA Cup on 18 occasions.

FAIRS CUP. This European competition, now known as the UEFA Cup, began its life in 1955 as the Industrial Fairs Cup. A team representing London were England's first participants, beaten 8–2 on aggregate by Barcelona in the final. United participated in the old Fairs Cup just once, in 1964–65, reaching the semi-finals where they were beaten after a play-off by Ferencvaros.

FAMILIES. United have had a number of families play for the club over the years, the most famous being John Aston senior and his son John Aston junior. Father played immediately after the war while his son was a member of United's European Cup winning side of 1968. There is also a family link today with the current manager's son, Darren Ferguson, fast becoming a regular first-team player. The two brothers Jimmy and Brian Greenhoff also played in the same United side during the 1970s.

FERGUSON, ALEX. Took over as United manager in November 1986 following the sacking of Ron Atkinson and has now served the longest spell as a United manager since

Alex Ferguson

Matt Busby. A former St Mirren and Glasgow Rangers player, Ferguson first went into management with East Stirling where he had the briefest of stays and then St Mirren, winding up at Aberdeen in 1978. Up to that point Ferguson was hardly a household name although he did take St Mirren to the first division championship. At Pittodrie he not only put the name of Aberdeen on the soccer map but his own as well, as his side went on to prove its quality across Europe. During his stay Aberdeen landed the Scottish title three times, the Scottish Cup four times and the League Cup on one occasion. But as well as those domestic honours, Ferguson's greatest prize was the winning of the European Cup-Winners' Cup. By then he was being tempted south of the Border by a number of English clubs but it was not until United came along that he finally succumbed to the challenge. A tough, no-nonsense disciplinarian, Ferguson had moulded a fine side together at

Pittodrie on the scantest of resources, a side always prepared to play attractive football. And it was a philosophy that he carried with him to Old Trafford. Young players were given their chances as he encouraged a return to the old days with the development of a youth policy. The most successful product of this policy has been Ryan Giggs who proved that you don't have to spend millions in the transfer market to find quality. But that was not to say that Ferguson shunned the big signings. On the contrary, he has always been prepared to spend in order to realise his ambitions with millions lashed out on Brian McClair, Mark Hughes, Roy Keane, Paul Ince, Neil Webb, Michael Phelan, Gary Pallister and the enigmatic Eric Cantona. It took time – at one point Ferguson's future at Old Trafford looked in doubt – but in the end it all began to pay dividends. Four years after joining United, Ferguson tasted his first success when United won the FA Cup. The following year they picked up the European Cup-Winners' Cup, and then went on to lift the European Super Cup and the League Cup. Then in May 1993 came the latest accolade. After 26 years the league championship returned to Old Trafford, making Alex Ferguson the first manager to win the title in both Scotland and England.

FERGUSON, DARREN. Son of manager Alex Ferguson. Made his debut for United as a substitute for Neil Webb at Bramall Lane in February 1991. Born in Glasgow in 1972, midfielder Darren Ferguson has all the hallmarks of his father. Strong, tenacious and not afraid to tackle, he is expected to figure prominently in United's future plans. Already a Scottish Under-21 international.

FEWEST DEFEATS. United's record for the fewest defeats in a season is four. This was achieved during the 1905–06 season as they finished runners up in the second division to win promotion.

FITZPATRICK, JOHN. Although John Fitzpatrick was

born in Aberdeen he came to prominence through United's youth ranks and was a member of the side that won the Youth Cup in 1964, playing alongside the likes of George Best, David Sadler, John Aston and Jimmy Rimmer. But astonishingly it would be the only honour he would ever win at Old Trafford despite nine years of first-team football. Most of the glory years would pass Fitzpatrick by as he battled against injury. A strong half-back, who was later to excel as a full-back, Fitzpatrick made his league debut in February 1965 against Sunderland but it was to be the first of only a handful of appearances during the next three seasons. He finally broke into the side during the 1967–68 season but managed only two appearances in United's European Cup run and was not in the side that played at Wembley. The following season, however, proved to be more satisfying as he made 28 league appearances and enjoyed a few more outings in Europe. That seemed to establish Fitzpatrick and over the next two years he made 69 appearances for United. But then, at the beginning of the 1971–72 season, disaster struck with an injury that was to put him on the sidelines for a year and eventually end his career. When he returned at the beginning of the following season it was to be for just one month as recurring injury once more sidelined him, this time forever. There was to be no comeback and at the age of 26 the young Scotsman gave up the relentless battle against injury and quit the game, returning to his native Scotland.

FLOODLIGHTS. United's floodlights were officially switched on for the first time on 25 March 1957 as United entertained Bolton Wanderers in a first division fixture. A crowd of 60,862, the largest of the season, turned up only to see United lose 2–0.

FOOTBALL LEAGUE. United became members of the Football League at the start of the 1892–93 season. Immediately prior to that, they played in the Football Alliance.

FOOTBALL LEAGUE CUP. United first appeared in the Football League Cup on 19 October 1960, earning a 1–1 draw at Exeter. After that season they shunned the competition for six years, reappearing in 1966, only to be beaten 5–1 at Blackpool. That led to a further boycotting of the competition but they reappeared again in September 1969 to beat Middlesbrough 1–0. Since then they have participated every year, appearing in three finals but winning the trophy just once, during the 1991–92 season.
Final Appearances:
1983 v Liverpool (Wembley) 1–2 (*aet*)
1991 v Sheffield Wednesday (Wembley) 0–1
1992 v Nottingham Forest (Wembley) 1–0

FOOTBALLER OF THE YEAR. The Football Writers' Footballer of the Year award has been won by United players on three occasions:
1948–49 Johnny Carey
1965–66 Bobby Charlton
1967–68 George Best
    The Professional Football Association award for Player of the Year has also gone to a number of United players:
1989 Mark Hughes
1991 Mark Hughes
1992 Gary Pallister
    The PFA award for Young Player of the Year has also gone to a number of United players:
1985 Mark Hughes
1991 Lee Sharpe
1992 Ryan Giggs
1993 Ryan Giggs

FORSYTH, ALEX. Tenacious defender during the Docherty era. Forsyth signed for United in January 1973, joining the club from Partick Thistle for £100,000. Ironically, he made his United debut against Arsenal, the club that six years earlier had let him go. Returning to Scotland, he had resurrected his flagging career with Partick where he won a

League Cup winners' medal. Forsyth had already come to the attention of Docherty during his short spell as manager of the Scottish national side and although his transfer to Old Trafford might have been something of a gamble, at £100,000 it was worth the risk. But Forsyth proved to be no gamble. From the start he was an assured, stylish and tough defender who had enough pace and skill to make confident runs forward. Forsyth enjoyed six seasons at United, making a total of 116/3 appearances, even scoring five goals. He won a second division championship medal with United in 1974–75 and a year later played in United's losing Cup final side. After that he lost his place to Jimmy Nicholl and played only three times the following season. The writing was on the wall and during the 1977–78 season, after just three more appearances, he eventually signed for Glasgow Rangers, where he had enjoyed a loan spell, and later played with Motherwell. Already a Scottish international with four caps by the time he arrived at Old Trafford, Forsyth went on to collect a further six caps.

FOULKES, BILL. One of the club's finest servants is perhaps the best way to describe Billy Foulkes with his 679/3 appearances in 18 seasons at Old Trafford. Only Bobby Charlton has played more games for the club. The careers of Foulkes and Charlton were linked in many ways. Both were Busby Babes, both survived the Munich disaster and both appeared in United's European Cup winning side. When his career ended in 1970 Foulkes could boast four championship medals, a European Cup winners' medal, an FA Cup winners' medal and four losers' medals, making him one of the most honoured players in United's history. Tall, strong, a fine header of the ball and a powerful runner, Foulkes was always the man to have in the heart of your defence. There was little that sneaked past him and he led by example. Born in St Helens in 1932, he first came to Old Trafford in 1949 as a schoolboy, turning professional two years later. He made his debut in December 1952 at Anfield and a week later held on to his place for the game at Chelsea but then had to wait until the following season for his next appearance. But the wait was worthwhile and from then on he only lost out through injury. Foulkes was a member of United's two title-winning sides of the mid-1950s as well as United's two losing Cup final teams. Then came Munich from which Foulkes miraculously escaped with only minor injuries. Astonishingly he was back playing football by the next week, lining up in United's team to play Sheffield Wednesday in the fifth round of the FA Cup. Foulkes also played at Wembley that year, captaining the side, as United lost to Bolton. But the traumas of the 1950s gave way to glory in the 1960s as United, powered by Best, Law and Charlton upfront, could play their brand of confident attacking football in the sure knowledge that with Foulkes behind them there was little to fear. He even scored the goal against Real Madrid that put United through to the European Cup final. At Wembley he captained United's European Cup winning side and remained with the club until 1970 by which time age and injury were beginning to catch up with him. At the end of that season he quit first-team football to take on a coaching job at the club. He later had coaching periods in Norway and the United States. Yet for all his appearances and for all his medals, Foulkes was only honoured once by his country and that was in 1954 when he appeared for England against Northern Ireland.

G

GASKELL, DAVID. United goalkeeper who joined the club in 1957. For many years he was understudy to Harry Gregg, making only the occasional appearance. Although his occasional appearances eventually mounted up, he was rarely automatic choice but he did total 118 games for the club. The arrival of Alex Stepney in 1966 put even more pressure on him and a few years later he moved to Wrexham where he played for a couple of seasons before retiring. Gaskell was capped at England schoolboy and youth level.

GIANTKILLERS. United are one of the biggest scalps in football and although they have not been embarrassed too many times in the FA Cup, there have been a few occasions which they might prefer to forget about. During the 1955–56 season, United, destined to win the title that season, went out at the first hurdle, beaten 0–4 at Bristol Rovers. Then in 1958–59 came one of the biggest shocks of all when giantkillers Norwich of the third division beat them 3–0 at Carrow Road. In 1983–84 it was a third division side again that claimed United's scalp, this time Bournemouth, who provided the shock of the round with a 2–0 hammering of United at Bournemouth.

GIBSON, COLIN. Signed by Ron Atkinson from Aston Villa for £275,000 in an attempt to give the club more left-back options. Gibson began promisingly but then tore his hamstring for a second time at the beginning of the 1986–87 season. In all, it took him 16 months to overcome his various injury problems but although he eventually returned to reclaim his place, the arrival of Denis Irwin and Paul Parker, plus the emergence of Lee Martin restricted his appearances. Gibson played just over 80 games for the club.

GIBSON, JAMES. United chairman for many years and the man responsible for saving the club when it faced financial ruin in 1931. Gibson was a successful Manchester business-man with a clothing firm. At the time United were at one of their lowest points both on and off the park and Gibson stepped in with an immediate £2,000 to guarantee players' wages and other administrative costs. He then made a further £20,000 available to help buy new players. It was Gibson as chairman who also agreed to set up a junior youth team as long ago as 1938. And it was Gibson who was instrumental in persuading the board that Matt Busby was the right man to become manager in 1945. His son Alan was also a director of the club, serving for 36 years, 28 of which were as vice-chairman.

GIBSON, TERRY. Joined United in 1985 from Coventry, having previously played with Tottenham, in a deal that took Alan Brazil to Highfield Road. A slightly built winger with a good burst of speed, his days at Old Trafford were interrupted by injury and inconsistency. He played just 23 league games before joining Wimbledon.

GIDMAN, JOHN. Although he was born in Liverpool, it was Aston Villa who first spotted the talents of John Gidman. He served his apprenticeship and early career with the Midlands club before signing for Everton in October 1979. By then he was already an England youth and under-23 international and the holder of a League Cup winners' medal. After a couple of seasons at Goodison he joined United in a swap deal that took Mickey Thomas to Merseyside. Gidman immediately slotted into the United defence, making 36 league appearances in his first season. After that he had mixed fortunes: injuries struck, he almost lost an eye in a fireworks accident, and he enjoyed only a handful of outings over the next couple of years. But he bravely fought back to regain his place for the 1984–85 season. He was a member of United's Cup winning line-up against his former club, Everton. At the end of the following season he was given a free transfer and although he enjoyed a temporary recall he eventually moved to Manchester City and then had spells with Stoke and Darlington where he became assistant manager.

GIGGS, RYAN. Talented young winger who made the eventual breakthrough into the United side during the 1992–93 season with some headline-hitting performances. Fast, skilful and strong, Giggs was soon being compared with George Best. Although he was born in Cardiff in November 1973, Giggs was brought up in the Manchester area and was actually at Manchester City's School of Excellence before United snapped him up as a trainee in July 1990. Four months later he signed professional forms. Four months after that he made his first-team debut against Everton at Old Trafford. He was still only 18 years old. Yet despite all the obvious talent United were careful to develop Giggs slowly, reluctant to throw him in to the first team week after week and it was not until 1992 that he became a permanent fixture in the United line-up. By then, his goals and tricky running had made it impossible to leave him out. He made his first appearance for Wales as a substitute against Germany in 1992 and his full-team debut a year later in the World Cup qualifier against Belgium when he slammed a free kick from outside the area into the roof of

Ryan Giggs

the net for Wales's opening goal. Giggs is now the most talked-about young player in the game. Already a twice winner of the PFA's Young Player of the Year award and a holder of a League Cup winners' medal and Youth Cup winners' medal, he is expected to become one of the game's leading players over the next few years. He won a championship medal with United in 1993 with some electrifying performances that saw him score nine league goals and link up so effectively with Eric Cantona.

GILES, JOHNNY. Given Giles's subsequent career after leaving Old Trafford there is little doubt that United let him move somewhat prematurely. Dublin-born Giles had come to United from the Irish club Home Farm as a 17-year-old in 1957. He made his league debut two years later, in September 1959, as United crashed 1–5 at home to Spurs. It was hardly an illustrious beginning and Albert Quixall was back for the following game. But he clearly did enough to impress and by the end of the season was enjoying a regular run out. In his four seasons at Old Trafford Giles made 99 league appearances, usually in the United midfield, scoring ten league goals. His final game was against Leicester City in the 1963 Cup final. Three months later he joined Leeds United in a £37,000 deal and began a career that would bring him countless honours including league championships, FA Cup medals and European success as well as 60 caps for the Republic of Ireland. When he retired from playing it was to take up management and he enjoyed successful spells with West Brom, and the Republic of Ireland.

GOALS. The most goals United have ever scored in one game were the 14 against Walsall in 1895 but as that match was later declared null and void the result did not stand. So officially the most goals United have ever scored are the ten against Anderlecht in the European Cup on 26 September 1956 and the ten against Wolves in the league in October 1892.

GOALS – INDIVIDUAL. The best individual performance by a United player in any game was that by George Best who scored six goals in February 1970 as United beat Northampton Town 8–2 in the fifth round of the FA Cup. Jack Rowley once scored seven goals for the club as they beat New Brighton but that was during the war when results had little meaning.

GOALS – HIGHEST. United's all-time highest goalscorer is Bobby Charlton with 247 goals in all matches. The top six goalscorers in United's history are:
Bobby Charlton 247
Denis Law 236
Jack Rowley 208
George Best 178
Dennis Viollet 178
Joe Spence 168

GOALS – HIGHEST, LEAGUE. United's leading league goalscorer is Bobby Charlton with 199 goals. The top six United league goalscorers are:
Bobby Charlton 199
Jack Rowley 182
Denis Law 171
Dennis Viollet 159
Joe Spence 158
George Best 137

GOALS – SEASON, LEAGUE. United's highest goalscorer in any single season is Dennis Viollet who scored 32 league goals during the 1959–60 season.

GOALS – SEASON, TOTAL. The highest number of goals scored by any United player in all competitions during a season is 46 goals, scored by Denis Law during the 1963–64 season. Thirty of them came in the league, ten in the FA Cup and six in Europe.

GOALKEEPERS. United once played three different goal-keepers in a match. The occasion was in January 1893 when they met Stoke in a first division fixture. Their regular goalkeeper, Warner, missed the train so United were forced to field a substitute keeper. Stewart, Fitzsimmons and Clements all took it in turns to have a go between the posts but it turned out to be something of a disaster as United lost 1–7.

GOLF. Today's footballers are well known for their golfing but back in 1977 United boasted the English amateur golf champion on their books. His name was Terry Shingler, a one-time Busby Babe. Unfortunately Shingler never managed a first-team outing, perhaps spending too much time on the links.

GOODWIN, FREDDIE. United half-back of the 1950s and also Lancashire cricketer. Goodwin came to Old Trafford in 1953 at the age of 20 and made his league debut in November 1954 against Arsenal. A half-back who could play on either the right or left, he was always overshadowed by stars such as Duncan Edwards and Eddie Coleman and consequently appearances were rare. After the Munich disaster, however, he was immediately drafted into the side and soon became a key member. He played in the 1958 Cup final and continued as a regular until Maurice Setters's arrival spelt the end of his Old Trafford career. The result was a move to Leeds United in March 1960 for £10,000 but with Leeds relegated almost immediately it was not to be a particularly fruitful relationship. A few years later he moved to Scunthorpe, missing out on the Leeds revival, and later had a spell as manager at Scunthorpe. Goodwin was probably to have more success as a manager, having useful periods at Brighton and Birmingham as well as in the United States. He was also a keen cricketer and enjoyed 11 first-class outings with Lancashire, scoring just 47 runs but taking 27 wickets at an average of 26.48 runs apiece.

GOWLING, ALAN. Joined United as a youngster and made his league debut in March 1968, taking over from the injured Denis Law to play alongside Best and Charlton and even scoring. He won England schoolboy, England amateur and England Under-23 international honours while he was with United. A tall, gangly striker who was born in Stockport, he never scored as many goals as might have been expected, netting just 21 in more than 80 appearances and was for a time converted into a midfielder. In June 1972 he was transferred to Huddersfield Town for £60,000 and suddenly began to show his worth, scoring 58 goals in 128 games. He later had spells with Newcastle where he successfully linked up with Malcolm Macdonald and at Bolton Wanderers where he formed a memorable striking partnership with Frank Worthington. He was educated at Manchester University while he was with United.

GREAT BRITAIN. Over the years a number of United amateurs have played soccer for Great Britain. The most prominent was Harold Hardman, later to become chairman of the club. Hardman represented Great Britain during the 1908 Olympic Games, playing three games and winning a gold medal. Other England amateur internationals have included J.Bradbury, Warren Bradley, M. Pinner and J. Walton.

GREENHOFF, BRIAN. Unlike his elder brother, Jimmy, Brian Greenhoff came to United as an apprentice, turning professional in June 1970. He had to wait three more years, however, for his first-team debut but once he had made the breakthrough he was there for the next six years, making 267 appearances and scoring 17 goals. He was a member of United's Cup winning side of 1977 as well as United's relegation and promotion sides of the early 1970s. Capped 17 times by England while at United, he made his debut against Wales in 1976. In 1979 he was transferred to Leeds United for £350,000 where he won another England cap. He later had spells with Hull City and Rochdale.

GREENHOFF, JIMMY. Elder brother of Brian Greenhoff. Born in Barnsley like his brother, he started his career with Leeds United before joining Birmingham and then Stoke. In November 1976 he came to United in a £100,000 transfer deal to lend some experience and weight to Tommy Docherty's emerging side. He scored the winning goal in the 1977 Cup final against Liverpool and appeared again at Wembley two years later as United went down to Arsenal. He played a total of 118/4 games for United, netting 36 goals. After five seasons at Old Trafford he moved to Crewe. He won England honours at Under-23 level but surprisingly was never capped at full international level.

GREGG, HARRY. Popular and outstanding goalkeeper of the 1950s and 60s. Born in Northern Ireland, Gregg came to Old Trafford from Doncaster Rovers in December 1957 for a record fee for a goalkeeper of £23,500. He was already a Northern Ireland international when he arrived at Old Trafford and went on to win a total of 25 caps. Gregg immediately took over in the United goal from Ray Wood and would eventually make 247 appearances for the club over the next nine seasons. Gregg survived the Munich disaster where he will always be remembered as one of the heroes who helped pull the injured from the wreckage. He was back in the United side immediately after the disaster, appearing against Sheffield Wednesday in the FA Cup and then in the final against Bolton where he was controversially bundled over the line by Nat Lofthouse for Bolton's second goal. He remained at Old Trafford until 1966 when David Gaskell replaced him in goal. From United he went to Stoke and then turned his hand to management, having useful spells with Shrewsbury, Swansea and Crewe. An agile and safe keeper, Gregg was also brave and determined, enjoying enormous success in the 1958 World Cup finals when he helped Northern Ireland into the quarter-finals.

GRIFFITHS, JOHN. Full-back who played with United

during their yo-yo years of the 1930s. He came to Old Trafford from Bolton Wanderers in 1934 as an emergency buy and was immediately drafted into the first team as United fought to stave off relegation to the third division. Griffiths proved to be worth his fee as United clung on to their second division spot. He remained with the club throughout the war years until 1945 when he joined Hyde United.

GRIMES, ASHLEY. Born in Dublin, he came to United from the Irish club Bohemians. He made his United debut in 1977 and went on to play 100 games for the club between then and 1982, scoring 11 goals. His best season was 1979–80 when he made 20 appearances in the United midfield and came on as a substitute in a further half dozen games as United stormed to the second division championship. He was sold to Coventry City in 1982 and later played with Luton Town.

GRIMWOOD, JOHN. United half-back of the inter-war years with almost 200 league appearances to his name. Born in the North East, Grimwood joined United during the First World War but had to wait until October 1919 for his first appearance, against Manchester City at Maine Road. Even then he was still only 19 years old. By the end of the season Grimwood was a regular and continued serving the club until 1927 when he was transferred to Aldershot. He later had a spell with Blackpool. His only honour was as a member of United's second division promotion side in 1925.

GUEST PLAYERS. During the Second World War league clubs were allowed to field guest players from local barracks as it was often difficult to obtain leave every week for their own players who might be barracked many miles away. Among those who guested for United were Harry Catterick, Ivor Broadis and Billy Liddell.

H

HALSE, HAROLD. Part of a famous United forward line of the Edwardian era that included Billy Meredith and Sandy Turnbull. Halse joined United in the summer of 1907 from Southend after having had spells with Wanstead, Barking and Clapton Orient. He was widely regarded as a scheming inside-foward, always ready to snap up opportunities and with the likes of Meredith and Turnbull around there were always going to be plenty at United. He played five seasons with the club, making 124 appearances and scoring 50 goals. In his first season he won a league championship medal and the following season an FA Cup winners' medal. Then in 1911 he picked up his second league championship medal. In July 1912 he left the club to join Aston Villa where he added a second FA Cup winners' medal to his collection and a league runners up medal, both in the same season. The following year he moved to Chelsea where he made his third Cup final appearance though this time he finished up on the losing side. He remained with Chelsea throughout the First World War, finally moving to Charlton in 1921 for a couple of seasons. He also made a total of four appearances for the Football League but surprisingly he was capped only once by England, winning his cap as a

United player in 1909. Surprising also because Halse scored twice as England thrashed Austria 8–1.

HANSON, JAMES. Manchester-born centre-forward of the inter-war years. Hanson joined United in 1924, scoring on his debut in November of that year as United faced Hull City. He had just reached his twentieth birthday. He scored in his next two outings but then had to make way for Bill Henderson, United's regular choice upfront who returned from injury. Henderson was to keep Hanson out of the side for some time but the following season Hanson finally made the breakthrough, playing 26 times but scoring only five goals. The goals were slow to come and in some ways it was a wonder United persevered but eventually they did arrive: 14 in the 1927–28 season and 20 the following season. Then, just as Hanson seemed to be maturing into a prolific goalscorer, he was injured and never played again. In all he had played 147 games for the club, scoring 52 goals.

HARDMAN, HAROLD. One of the outstanding names in the club's history. Hardman served the club as player, director and, for many years, as chairman. And on top of all that he was also an Olympic gold medalist. Hardman played his early football, as an amateur, with Chorlton-cum-Hardy and Northern Nomads, before joining Everton in the summer of 1903. A short, wiry winger, he was an FA Cup winner with Everton and also won four England caps even though he was still an amateur. Then in 1908 he won his Olympic gold medal with the Great Britain soccer team at the London Olympics. Shortly after his Olympic success he joined United but made only four appearances for the club, all in his first season 1908–09. By January of 1909 he was on his way, this time choosing to play with Bradford City. A year later he joined Stoke and then in November 1912 returned to United to eventually become a director of the club. In 1951 he became chairman and remained in that post until his death in June 1965, seeing the club through the difficult years following Munich. Hardman was also a

Manchester-based solicitor.

HAT-TRICK HEROES. There have been many hat-trick heroes in United's long history but perhaps the most unusual was Charlie Mitten who in March 1950 scored a hat-trick of penalties as United thrashed Aston Villa 7–0. Mitten also scored another goal that day.

HAYES, VINCE. Another member of United's outstanding Edwardian side. Hayes began his career when the side were still known as Newton Heath, joining them in early 1901. He played just once that season but made 16 appearances the following campaign. He never really established himself, however, until 1903–04 when he reverted to his favourite position as a full-back. At the end of the 1904–05 season, after losing his place, he moved to Brentford but as the 1908–09 season kicked off Hayes moved back to United, regained his old place, and was a member of the club's Cup winning side. He had already missed out on United's league championship side and was to miss out again in 1910–11 as United won the title for a second time with Hayes making just one appearance. At the end of that season, after 128 games for the club, he moved to Bradford Park Avenue and later had a spell as manager of Preston North End.

HERD, DAVID. It was strange that both Manchester United and Manchester City should have allowed young David Herd to slip through their scouting nets. After all, his father was the well-known Alec Herd who had starred with Manchester City, and son David began his football with Stockport County. But neither City nor United seemed interested in him and in 1954 he was snapped up by Arsenal. By 1956 he had won a regular place in the Gunners' side and went on to score 143 goals for them, at the rate of more than one every two games. It also won him international recognition with five Scottish caps. United finally realised the error of their ways in the summer of 1961 and paid £35,000 for him. And he proved to be a most valuable signing. In his seven seasons at Old Trafford he brought experience and goals to the side, managing 20 goals a season on four occasions and scoring 32 goals in the 1965–66 season. He scored twice in the 1963 Cup final as United beat Leicester and he was a vital part of the championship-winning sides of 1965 and 1967. The following year he played a few games in Europe but by then age was beginning to catch up with him and after missing out on the European Cup final he decided to leave Old Trafford. He initially joined Stoke but after a brief spell left them to play with Waterford in the League of Ireland. One of his great distinctions is to be among the rare players to have played league football alongside their father when both he and Alec Herd turned out for Stockport in the final game of the 1950–51 season.

HIGGINS, MARK. Former Everton captain who had been forced to retire early because of injury. Higgins, however, fought his way back to fitness and United manager Ron Atkinson agreed to give him a second chance at Old Trafford. Higgins even paid back the insurance money he had received on his early retirement. But it was all to no avail. Higgins played just eight games for United, then had to admit that his injuries had caught up with him once again.

HILDITCH, CLARENCE. United player and manager. During the inter-war years there was little to cheer about at Old Trafford. United failed to win any major honours and had few outstanding players to boast about. But in Clarence Hilditch they at least had one player who could hold his own in any company. Hilditch was born near Nantwich and joined United from Altrincham during the First World War. But he did not make his United debut until the 1919–20 season when he went on to make 32 appearances. He was a centre-half; dependable, strong and a fine header of the ball. He had 16 seasons playing for United, making 322 outings but his only international honour was to play for England in the Victory international in 1919 and against South Africa in the 1920 Commonwealth internationals. Unfortunately neither counted as a full international. Hilditch captained United for many years and when manager John Chapman was suddenly suspended by the Football Association in 1924 it was not really surprising that the club should look to its most trusted servant to help them out. Hilditch was made player-manager, the only ever such appointment in the club's history. His time in charge, however, was not particularly successful. The side were already deep in trouble when he was appointed and it had been made clear to him that the job was only temporary. He had no authority to change things and was always reluctant to select himself. But he did manage to keep United in the first division, eventually handing over power to Herbert Bamlett when he was appointed manager at the end of the season. Hilditch, like the loyal man he was, gracefully stepped aside and continued with the task of playing for the club which he did until he retired in 1932.

HILL, GORDON. Tricky little winger who was a great favourite with the United crowd. He joined United in November 1975 after a successful couple of years with third division Millwall and was soon on the honours trail. Within a year he had played in the FA Cup final and had won Under-23 and full England honours. He later went on to make a total of six England appearances, three of those as substitute. In 1977 he was a member of United's Cup winning side as they sneaked a famous victory over Liverpool. Hill had cost United manager Tommy Docherty £70,000 but was to bring an excitement to Old Trafford that had been missing for many years. Hill liked to chase and harry down the flanks and his thrilling runs made United one of the most attractive sides in English football. He enjoyed just three seasons at Old Trafford, playing 132 games and scoring 51 goals, but then a dispute with the club led to them unloading him to Derby County for £250,000, then managed by Tommy Docherty. Eighteen months later he moved again, this time to QPR, signed once more by none other than Tommy Docherty. Hill ended his career playing football in the United States.

HINE, ERNEST. Another Barnsley product who found his way to Old Trafford. After five years with his local club, Barnsley, Hine joined Leicester City in 1926 and went on to establish himself as one of the best centre-forwards of his era. Leicester came within a whisker of the league title and Hine won six England caps. He won his first cap in 1929, having already played for the Football League on three occasions. His final two appearances for England came in 1932 shortly before he left Leicester to join Huddersfield Town. But he remained at Huddersfield for less than a year, joining United in February 1933. After Leicester his goalscoring touch seemed to desert him and he stayed at Old Trafford for just 22 months. He had played 53 games but had found the net only 12 times. He was already 32 by the time United signed him and had clearly seen his best days. In December 1934 he returned to Barnsley.

HOGG, GRAEME. Born in Aberdeen, Hogg came to United as an apprentice. He had a disastrous start to his career with United, making his first-team debut against Bournemouth in the third round of the FA Cup in January 1984. United lost 0–2 in one of the biggest Cup upsets for years. But despite the headline-hitting defeat, Hogg was not discarded and went on to play more than 100 games for the club before new manager Alex Ferguson sold him to Portsmouth. He also had a lean spell at West Bromwich Albion before moving to Hearts.

HOLDEN, DICK. Defender who played with United during the early years of the twentieth century. Local-born Holden made his debut in the final match of the 1904–05 season and then became a regular the following season. He won a championship medal in 1907–08 but then lost his place and missed out on the FA Cup run the following season. He won a second championship medal in 1911 although he only made eight appearances that season. Two years later a persistent knee injury forced his retirement. He played 17 games.

HOLTON, JIM. 'Six foot two, eyes of blue, Big Jim Holton's after you!' sang the Stretford End. Holton was a great favourite at United as they stormed to the second division championship. As rugged as they come, dependable and the mainstay of a fine United defence, Holton was one of Tommy Docherty's first signings, bought from Shrewsbury Town for £80,000 in 1973. He was a giant of a centre-half who towered over many of his colleagues and must have frightened the wits out of many a striker. But against Sheffield Wednesday in early December 1975 he broke a leg and never played first-team football again for the club. In a pre-season friendly eight months later he was all set for a return but in the pre-match kick-in he twisted his knee and had to limp off before the game had even begun. Holton recovered fairly quickly but a few weeks later, playing for the reserves, he tragically broke his leg again. It marked the end of his United days and later that year he was transferred to Sunderland. He had played just 69 games for the club. But Holton was always a determined character and despite his injuries he clawed his way back to fitness with Sunderland and later had spells with Coventry and Sheffield Wednesday. Holton was capped 15 times by Scotland, winning his first cap in 1973 against Wales.

HOME RECORD. United's best ever home record was in the 1955–56 season when they won 18 of their 21 games, drawing the other three, and scoring 51 goals and conceding 20. United have gone unbeaten at home over a season on five occasions.

HOUSTON, STEWART. Another of Tommy Docherty's famous Scottish charges. Docherty first signed Houston for Chelsea back in August 1967 but when Docherty quit

Stamford Bridge a short time later Houston never made the grade and drifted to Brentford. And it was from there that Docherty signed him for a second time, this time for United. That was in December 1973 and Houston cost the club £55,000. Houston made his debut immediately in what turned out to be George Best's final game and went on to give seven valuable years' service to United with 248/2 games. United were relegated in his first season but the following year he collected a second division championship medal. In 1976 he was on the losing side in the FA Cup final and a year later missed out through injury as United lifted the cup. He was capped by Scotland just once, playing against Denmark in 1976. He was given a free transfer during the summer of 1980 and opted to join Sheffield United where he played for three years before joining Colchester.

HUGHES, MARK. One of the all-time United favourites who has a habit of scoring sensational goals. Hughes came to Old Trafford as a youngster and played with the youth side that lost the 1982 FA Youth Cup final. He made his first-team debut against Port Vale in the League Cup in October 1983 but had to wait another six months before his league baptism. He scored in his first match against Leicester and since then has been an automatic choice. Tall, powerful and dangerous in the box, Hughes is a handful for any defender. He has a ferocious shot and as spectacular a volley as anything Old Trafford has ever seen. And there were few better examples than the volley he sent thundering into the Liverpool net in the League Cup in October 1990 at Old Trafford. In his first full season with the team he collected a Cup winners' medal after beating Everton at Wembley. It was little wonder that Hughes soon had every scout in Europe coming to Old Trafford to see his talents. In the end a move to the continent was inevitable with Barcelona scooping the prize for £2.3 million. But Spain proved to be a different proposition to the Football League. Goals were even harder to come by and the club even more

Mark Hughes

demanding. For a while he was loaned out to Bayern Munich where his old sharpshooting and enthusiasm were rekindled. A move back to Old Trafford was always on the cards and in June 1988 he duly returned for £1.5 million. Since then Hughes has shown his hunger for the game once more, helping United to every honour, including the league championship. He added a second FA Cup winners' medal to his collection in 1990 as United beat Crystal Palace, Hughes hitting a couple in the first drawn game. He also collected winners' medals in the League Cup in 1992 and the European Cup-Winners' Cup where his two goals settled the match against his former colleagues Barcelona. It was sweet revenge for him. He won his first Welsh cap in 1984 and now has almost 50 caps to his name. He won the award for PFA Young Player of the Year in 1985 and has since been named PFA Player of the Year on two occasions – 1989 and 1991.

HUNDRED GOALS. United have scored more than 100 league goals in a season on three occasions. The first time was in the 1956–57 season when they struck 103 goals to win the championship. They then scored the same number of goals two seasons later in 1958–59 but only finished second. In 1959–60 they scored 102 goals, finishing in seventh spot.

HUNDRED THOUSAND. United's first £100,000 player was Denis Law, signed from Torino of Italy in 1962 for £115,000. It was the first time any British club had ever paid a six-figure fee for a player.

I

INCE, PAUL. Midfielder signed from West Ham United in August 1989 for a fee of £1 million. For a time it had seemed that Ince's much publicised transfer to United was about to fall through after he had failed his medical. Two weeks later, however, an independent medical panel reported that his pelvic problem was not quite as serious as had initially been diagnosed. The transfer fee was duly reduced from £2 million to £1 million and Ince had his wish to become a United player. He had made 72 appearances for West Ham, scoring seven goals. Although he was already an England Under-21 international when he joined United it was to be a few more years before he added full England honours to his collection. He won his first England cap under Graham Taylor and looks set to be a pillar of the England midfield as well as United's. Ince began slowly at Old Trafford but has matured into a strong-running midfielder who likes to get into the penalty area and into scoring positions, taking over the Bryan Robson role. He was a member of United's European Cup-Winners' Cup side that defeated Barcelona in the final and was also a medal winner in the League Cup Final against Nottingham Forest. But above all he will be remembered for his part in

Paul Ince

United's championship-winning side of 1992–93 when his forceful runs and goals swung the title in United's direction. He has now made more than 150 appearances for United.

INTER-CLUB TRANSFERS. Since the war there have been a number of notable transfer deals between the two big Manchester clubs with City generally coming off better. Perhaps the most memorable was the transfer of Denis Law from United to City in July 1973. One transfer the other way was the signing of Wyn Davies from City by United. Unfortunately Davies did not last very long at Old Trafford. One man who had two transfers between the Manchester clubs was Billy Meredith: he joined United from City in May 1906 and then returned to City in July 1921.

INTER-LEAGUE MATCHES. The first Inter-League match staged by United was in April 1904 at their Bank Street ground when the Football League beat the Scottish League 2–1. The next game was at Old Trafford in September 1912 when the Football League beat the Southern League. Old Trafford then had to wait until November 1961 for another game when the Football League lost 0–2 to the Italian League. Old Trafford also hosted an official benefit game organised by the Football League for the late John Robson played between two representative sides.

INTERNATIONAL CAPS – FIRST. The distinction of being the first United player to be capped by their country falls to two men, Jack Powell and T. Burke who both played for Wales against England in February 1887.

INTERNATIONAL CAPS – MOST. The most capped United player is, of course, Bobby Charlton who won 106 England caps.

INTERNATIONAL MATCHES. Old Trafford has staged a number of international matches. The first was in April

1926 when England lost 0–1 to Scotland. During the 1966 World Cup finals Old Trafford hosted three games involving Bulgaria, Hungary and Portugal.

IRWIN, DENIS. Signed from Oldham Athletic in June 1990. Irwin began his footballing days with Leeds United but was allowed to join Oldham for the knock-down price of £60,000 in May 1986 after just 72 league appearances. At Boundary Park, however, his career started to take off and he soon began to realise the potential that had already brought him Irish Under-21 and youth honours. But it took a move to Old Trafford before he finally broke into the full international ranks. He won his first Irish cap in 1991 against Morocco and has so far added another dozen to his collection. A right-back with a sure tackle, Irwin also likes to get forward and his accurate crosses have resulted in numerous opportunies for United's tall attackers. Irwin's biting tackles have helped make United's defence the meanest in the Premier league. He won a championship medal in 1992–93 and has also picked up a European Cup-Winners' Cup medal, a League Cup medal and a European Super Cup medal with United.

Denis Irwin

J

JAMES, STEVE. Although Steve James enjoyed seven years of first-team football at Old Trafford he was always in and out of the side. In the end he boasted just one full season of soccer, 1971–72, when he made 37 league appearances. For various reasons – injury, loss of form and competition – he could never quite establish himself as the automatic choice for the number five jersey. A strong, powerful centre-half, he made his first-team debut as a 19-year-old in October 1968 in front of 53,000 at Anfield, having joined United as a 16-year-old. By the end of that season he had notched up 21 league appearances, even managing a goal. It promised much for the future but the following season he was out of favour as newly signed Ian Ure stepped into his boots. James then had to wait until the 1971–72 season before he was back in contention. By then Ure had moved on and James was the only obvious replacement. But even that never lasted and at the end of the 1974–75 season he decided to move, joining York City. He had played seven seasons of football at Old Trafford yet had managed only 160 appearances. He played another 100 games at York before finally quitting the game in 1980.

JONES, MARK. Fearless, young centre-half killed in the Munich disaster. Like his fellow Busby Babe Tommy Taylor, Mark Jones was also born in Barnsley. But unlike Taylor, Jones was a United man from the start. He joined the club as a schoolboy, making his first appearance when he was only 17 years old in October 1950 against Sheffield Wednesday in front of more than 40,000 at Old Trafford. He managed just four outings that season and three the following season as United claimed the title. He may not have played too many times in his early years but when he did lay permanent claim to the number five shirt in the 1955–56 season United went on to clinch the championship. He was also a member of the championship-winning side the following season although he was to miss out on a Cup final place to Jackie Blanchflower. By then Blanchflower and Jones were locked in combat for the centre-half slot and during the 1957–58 season Jones made just 16 appearances before his tragic death at Munich. He had played in four of United's European Cup games that season, including the final match against Red Star. When he died, Jones was still only 25 although he seemed to have been around Old Trafford for years. He was a tough, natural centre-half who never over-complicated the game. It was surprising, given his importance to the two United championship sides, that he was never honoured by his country at a senior level though it was probably only the presence of Billy Wright which kept him out of contention.

JONES, TOM. Welsh international defender of the inter-war years. Born in North Wales, Jones joined United from Oswestry Town in 1925 and went on to give 11 years' loyal service before moving into non-league football. And yet despite his many years at Old Trafford, Jones only really established himself and was automatic choice in just a couple of those seasons. More often than not he was vying for one of the full-back positions with Charlie Moore, John Silcock and later, Billy Porter. But he never complained and even though they were lean years for the club, he remained ready to give of his best. In 1926 he was capped by Wales, making his international debut against Northern Ireland. He played twice more against the Irish and also against England during the next four years.

JORDAN, JOE. During the late 1970s there was no finer sight at Old Trafford than Joe Jordan in full flight. Brave, dashing and committed, Jordan was an old-fashioned type of centre-forward, always prepared to go in where others might have been less adventurous. What's more it paid off handsomely with 37 goals in 109 league appearances and an eventual transfer to AC Milan followed by a spell with Verona. Born in Scotland, Jordan began his footballing days with Morton before Leeds United paid £15,000 to bring him to Elland Road in October 1970 after he had made just ten league appearances. Within a couple of years Jordan was leading the Yorkshire side's assault on the league championship. He later played in two European finals before United lashed out a massive £350,000 on him. A few weeks later he was joined at Old Trafford by his former Leeds clubmate, Gordon McQueen. Jordan was new manager Dave Sexton's first signing and heralded the end of Stuart Pearson's career with United. Jordan immediately resumed his career as one of the most feared strikers in the first division and although he may not have netted as many goals as a striker should, his strength lay in his ability to unsettle defenders and pressurise goalkeepers. He was a strong header of the ball, could climb as high as any defender and was probably the strongest striker in the Football League. In all he played 125 games for United, hitting 41 goals. His best season was his last one, 1980–81, when he netted 15 goals in 33 league appearances. After his spell in Italy Jordan returned to England and picked up his career with Southampton. During his years with Leeds, Manchester United and AC Milan, Jordan was capped 52 times by Scotland in an international career that spanned almost ten years and three World Cup finals. He later moved to Bristol City, eventually becoming their manager where his success brought him the offer of a return north to manage Hearts. Jordan is now a coach with Celtic.

JOVANOVIC, NIKOLA. Yugoslav international signed by Dave Sexton in 1979 from Red Star Belgrade. Central defender Jovanovic was one of a number of Yugoslavs who suddenly descended on English football but it was a deal that never really worked out and after just 25 appearances he left United. His best moment had probably been his two goals in the 5–0 thrashing of Leicester City in September 1980. He was capped five times by Yugoslavia while he was a United player.

K

KANCHELSKIS, ANDREI. Ukrainian-born winger who joined United in May 1991 from the Soviet club Shakhytor Donetsk after leaving his country, following the fall of communism. Fast, sharp and direct, Kanchelskis was soon winning honours in Britain, helping United to the League Cup in 1992 and then to the league championship in 1993. With Giggs on one wing and Kanchelskis harrying on the other, United boasted a width that they had not enjoyed since the days of Gordon Hill and Steve Coppell. He has now played more than 50 league games for United and been capped by the Soviet Union on more than a dozen occasions since his arrival at Old Trafford.

KEANE, ROY. Young Irish international midfielder signed from Nottingham Forest for a Premier League record fee of £3.75m in July 1993. Keane had joined Forest from Cobh Ramblers during the 1990 close season. Yet despite his youth and inexperience he made 35 league appearances during his first season, playing in the Cup final against Spurs and winning his first full Irish cap. The following season he appeared in the League Cup final against United. Keane has pace and skill as well as imagination, and is expected to bring a touch of elegance to the United midfield.

KHAKI FINAL. This was the name given to the 1915 FA Cup final played at Old Trafford between Sheffield United and Chelsea. It became known as the Khaki final because of the many soldiers in uniform among the 50,000 crowd.

KIDD, BRIAN. Current assistant manager but best remembered for his United playing days and especially for his goal against Benfica in the 1968 European Cup final. Born in Manchester, Kidd joined United as a schoolboy, making his first-team debut in the Charity Shield against Tottenham at Old Trafford in August 1967. From that moment on Kidd was a regular choice, even though he was still only 18 years old. He played 38 league games in his first season, helping United towards second spot in the table with his 15 league goals. But it was his goal – United's third – scored on his nineteenth birthday, in the European Cup final against Benfica which sealed United's victory and Kidd's everlasting fame. It could so easily have been downhill all the way after that but Kidd was always a level-headed youngster and went on to enjoy many more years at Old Trafford. Over a period of seven seasons he made a total of 255/9 appearances, scoring 70 goals. Kidd was perhaps not as prolific as he should have been for a striker, only once managing 20 goals in a season at Old Trafford, yet to size him up on those statistics alone would be wrong. Kidd's contribution was considerable. His pace and strength put many a defender under pressure, allowing his fellow attackers more freedom and goal-scoring opportunities. Perhaps had he been more selfish he might have scored many more goals but that was not the Kidd style. He was capped twice by England, winning both caps in 1970, appearing against Northern Ireland and Ecuador. Four years later he was transferred to Arsenal for £110,000 and went on to score 30 league goals in 77 league appearances, a scoring rate which tempted Manchester City to bring him

Brian Kidd

back north in 1976 in another £100,000 move. Three years later, after a highly successful spell at Maine Road, he was on the move again, this time joining Everton for £150,000. He later played with Bolton and had a spell in the United States before returning to try his hand at coaching and management. He was appointed assistant manager at United in 1991 after Archie Knox had decided to move back to Scotland as assistant to Walter Smith at Glasgow Rangers.

KNIGHTON, MICHAEL. Businessman who tried to take over United during the autumn of 1989. In the end no deal was forthcoming and amid huge, and somewhat damaging, publicity Knighton withdrew although he was made a member of the board.

L

LAW, DENIS. Although he also played with Huddersfield Town, Torino and had a couple of spells with Manchester City, Denis Law will always be associated with United. He was part of a glorious era when United's attacking force of Best, Charlton and Law was the finest in Europe and one of the greatest in the club's history. Law was a prince among goalscorers. Born in Aberdeen, he came to Huddersfield Town as a youngster, signed by the then Huddersfield manager, the incomparable Bill Shankly. Law was soon among the headlines, with every club in Britain chasing his signature. Bill Shankly wanted to take him to Liverpool but his new club would not stump up the money. In March 1960 Manchester City came in with a record-breaking £55,000 offer that even Huddersfield could not refuse. A year later City were on the receiving end of a similar impossible-to-reject offer and Law was on his way to Italy, joining Torino for what was then a staggering £100,000. But the romance with Italian soccer soon turned sour and 12 months after his much-publicised arrival Matt Busby came sweeping to the rescue with another record-breaking deal that cost United £115,000. But it was to be money well spent. Over the next ten seasons Law would play 393/6 games for United,

Denis Law

scoring a staggering 236 goals, a rate of more than a goal every two games that would make him one of the most prolific goalscorers in the club's history. And without his continuing injuries his record would have been even more impressive. Law was majestic. He had a body swerve and an ability to hold and carry the ball into danger areas. He was also a goal poacher, ready to pounce and seize on any opportunities. And on top of this he could head the ball as well as anyone in the Football League. But above all Law had an appetite for the game that took him from one end of the field to the other in search of glory. He was a team player, blessed with individual skills, a modern-day Billy Meredith. In his time at Old Trafford he won an FA Cup winners' medal and two league championships but found himself in hospital as United lined up against Benfica in the 1968 European Cup final. He was also European Footballer of the Year in 1964 and made a total of 55 appearances for Scotland, 35 of these while he was with United, and scored a record 30 goals for his country. He also played for the Rest of the World against England and for the Italian League. Law's career with United came to a sad end in 1973 when he was given a free transfer by Tommy Docherty. The first Law heard of it was on television. It was not a way to treat a man who had given so much to the club. And so in July 1973 he rejoined Manchester City and nine months later, as United struggled at the bottom of the first division, he returned to Old Trafford and in the final minutes back-heeled the ball into the United net for a goal that would send United into the second division. Such irony.

LEAGUE GOALS – MOST SCORED. United's highest goal tally in the Football League was during the 1956–57 and 1958–59 seasons when they scored 103 goals on both occasions.

LEAGUE GOALS – LEAST CONCEDED. In the 1924–25 season United conceded just 23 goals, the best in the club's history.

LEAGUE GOALS – MOST IN A GAME. The highest number of league goals scored by United in any one game was ten in the 10–1 win over Wolverhampton Wanderers in a division two game in October 1892.

LEAGUE GOALS – MOST INDIVIDUAL. Dennis Viollet holds the United record for the most league goals in a season with 32 scored in the first division during the 1959–60 season.

LEAGUE GOALS – CAREER HIGHEST. Bobby Charlton holds the United record for the most number of goals with a career total of 199 goals between 1956 and 1973.

LEAGUE POINTS – HIGHEST. United's highest points total for a season is 84, achieved during their championship season 1992–93. But that total was amassed under the three points for a win system. Under the two points for a win rule their highest total is 64, achieved during the 1956–57 season when they won the championship.

LEIGHTON, JIM. Former Aberdeen goalkeeper who had shared many glorious years at Pittodrie with manager Alex Ferguson. Leighton played more than 250 games with the Dons, winning two league championship medals, four Scottish Cup medals and also a European Cup-Winners' Cup medal. Ferguson paid his old club a British record fee for a goalkeeper of £750,000 during the summer of 1988. At the time it seemed an excessive amount of money considering United already had two able keepers in Chris Turner and Gary Walsh. But Leighton went straight into the side and remained there for a couple of seasons until Les Sealey took over. Ferguson bought Leighton for his experience. He was already the holder of more than 40 Scottish caps and by the time his Old Trafford career was over he had a grand total of 58, making him one of the highest capped goalkeepers in the history of Scottish football. Leighton was an agile keeper but was prone to the

Jim Leighton

occasional lapse. After appearing in the FA Cup final against Crystal Palace he was then dropped for the replay and was left out of the side for the following season. It was clear that after 94 games he was no longer a part of Ferguson's long-term plans. He had loan spells with Arsenal and Reading before returning north of the Border to Dundee in February 1992 for £200,000 and is now with Hibernian.

LEITCH, ARCHIBALD. Noted architect of football grounds who was responsible for the original design of Old Trafford and the building of the ground between 1909 and 1910.

LITTLEWOODS CUP. See Football League Cup.

LOCHEAD, ANDY. Scottish inside-forward of the inter-war years. Lochead joined United from Hearts after just a handful of games for the Edinburgh club and made his debut as United crashed 0–5 to Everton in the opening match of the 1921–22 season. By the end of that season United were propping up the rest of the league. Lochead was unfortunate to be playing in what was a poor United side. Even in the second division, goals were hard to come by and at the end of his United career he had scored just 50 goals in 153 appearances. In October 1926, after five seasons at Old Trafford, he moved to Leicester City where his talents finally flourished as Leicester swept towards the top of the first division.

LONGEST GAME. United have been involved in some extraordinary long cup ties, but none surpass their epic struggle with Small Heath during the 1903–04 FA Cup. The two sides faced each other in the intermediate round of the Cup and in the first game at Clayton on 12 December they drew 1–1. Four days later they replayed at Small Heath where they again drew 1–1 after extra time. The second replay was held at Bramall Lane on 21 December where for the third time they drew one apiece, again after extra time. It was to take a fourth game to settle the affair. This time it was played on 11 January at Hyde Road in Manchester with United winning 3–1. The tie had taken 420 minutes to settle. When United won the FA Cup in 1989 it took them an extraordinary 13 games to reach Wembley. As if that was not enough, they then drew the first game against Crystal Palace before winning the replay. It had taken a total of 15 games to win the Cup.

M

MACARI, LOU. Celtic's Lou Macari looked all set to be joining Liverpool in January 1973 but after a visit to Anfield where he watched Liverpool beat Burnley in a cup tie he suddenly changed his mind. That alerted United manager Tommy Docherty and within days the young Scot was on his way to Old Trafford, costing the club a massive £200,000. And yet his United career was slow to take off. In his first season they narrowly missed being relegated and in his second neither he nor any other of United's expensive stars could save the side from the drop into the second division. Eventually, however, his talents began to shine and he went on to play 400 games for the club, scoring almost a century of goals. In Scotland, with Celtic, Macari had won two league championships and two Scottish Cups but although he never managed to add a league championship medal to his collection at United, he did win an FA Cup winners' medal and a losers' medal. Macari was a typical Scottish inside-forward: tenacious, hard-working and bubbling with skill. He won six Scottish caps while he was with Celtic and then added a further 18 to his collection while he was with United. He left United in 1984 to take over as player-manager of Swindon Town.

MacDOUGALL, TED. Prolific goalscorer with third division Bournemouth who signed for United amid much publicity in 1972 for £200,000. Although MacDougall had scored 103 goals in 146 outings for the south coast club, paying so much money for a third division striker was something of a gamble for new United manager Frank O'Farrell and it was a gamble that never paid off. MacDougall looked out of place in first division football although to be fair he was never really given much opportunity to find his feet. He played just 18 times, scoring five goals, before he was transferred to West Ham United. He was just as unfortunate there but finally settled at Norwich where his goalscoring touch returned. He later enjoyed a rewarding spell with Southampton. He was capped seven times by Scotland with all seven caps won while with Norwich.

MAINE ROAD. Home of Manchester City Football Club but also the home of United during the post-war seasons of 1946–47, 1947–48 and 1948–49. War damage at Old Trafford forced United to look for alternative accommodation until their own ground had been fully repaired and City obligingly lent them their ground. Consequently, United played all their home league fixtures at Maine Road as well as numerous Cup ties. When City were drawn at home in the Cup they had priority and United were forced to look even further afield. United finally returned to Old Trafford on 24 August 1949. Maine Road turned out to be something of a lucky ground for United and its huge capacity meant some bumper gates with 81,565 turning up to see United take on giantkillers Yeovil Town in February 1949. In the previous round 82,771 had watched them play Bradford. Maine Road also became United's home for a brief time during their first season in Europe. As United were still installing their floodlights they were forced to look elsewhere for a ground that already had floodlights. Fortunately they had to look no further than Maine Road. Again it meant some massive gates with 75,000 watching them play Borussia Dortmund and 70,000 seeing the memorable fight back against Athletico Bilbao in the next round.

MANGNALL, ERNEST. The first great United manager. Mangnall was a Bolton man, educated at the local grammar school, who became a supporter of Bolton Wanderers during their early years. Before long he had been appointed a director of the club, eventually becoming secretary. He was then lured away to perform the same job with Lancashire neighbours Burnley. He helped Burnley through a difficult financial patch and in September 1903 the United chairman J.J. Bentley recommended him for the job of secretary at United. In those days it was a very different role, more akin to that of manager. Mangnall chose the side, with a little help from the directors, and also bought and sold the players as well as looking after the administrative side of the club. Mangnall was to be an inspired choice, guiding the club from the depths of the second division to the top of the first division in just a few years. Under Mangnall United won two league titles and the FA Cup to become one of the most famous sides in Edwardian football. He even built a new stadium at Old Trafford to give his players and supporters the kind of facilities they deserved. Mangnall was a shrewd businessman who bought some fine players, and often very cheaply. He brought Billy Meredith to the club along with Charlie Roberts, Sandy Turnbull, Alex Bell and Dick Duckworth. But then in 1912 he sensationally quit the club to join Manchester City. It spelt the end of a glorious era for United and it would take them 30 years to recover. But for City it was the dawning of a new age. Eighteen months later they were top of the first division while United were bottom. Unfortunately war intervened and Mangnall's work at City was interrupted. Nevertheless he went on to build them a new stadium at Maine Road and remained with the club until 1924. He died in 1932.

MARTIN, LEE. Full-back who made his league debut for the club at the end of the 1987–88 season against Wimbledon. He began the following season in the first team but was then left out of the side until mid-November. When he returned it was for an extended run that took him through to the end of the 1990–91 season. Born in Manchester, Martin was a product of the United youth system and was a member of the side that reached the FA Youth Cup final in 1986. His moment of glory, however, came four years later when he appeared in the FA Cup final against Crystal Palace, scoring the winning goal in the replay. He generally played as a left-back but was equally at home in the other full-back berth. In recent years, however, injury and the arrival of Denis Irwin and Paul Parker have limited his opportunities. He has played over 70 games for the club and been capped twice at England Under-21 level.

Lee Martin

McBAIN, NEIL. Neil McBain may have played 43 games for United but deserves mention for his other great claim to fame, that of being the oldest player to ever appear in a Football League match. It came many years after he had left

United, in March 1947. By then he was managing New Brighton in the third division-north when an injury crisis struck. So the manager was forced to pull on the keeper's jersey and take his place between the posts. He was 51 years and four months old. It was also unusual because McBain was not a goalkeeper. At United he had been a half-back. He joined the club in November 1921 but after two years left to join Everton. He later had spells with St Johnstone, Liverpool and Watford. After that he turned to management with posts at Watford, Ayr United, Luton and Leyton Orient. And, as if he had not had a fascinating enough career, he ended his days as coach of the great Argentinian side Estudiantes. He won three Scottish caps, the first while he was with United against England in 1922.

McCLAIR, BRIAN. Since joining United in June 1987 Brian McClair has gone on to claim just about every medal the English game can offer. He came to United from Celtic for £850,000, already a proven goalscorer with 35 goals in his final season at Parkhead. Before that he had been with Motherwell. Although the net has proved more elusive in English football, McClair's strongest qualities are his strength and determination. He is a powerhouse as he thunders into opposing penalty areas, terrifying defenders and always ready to lay on goals for others. It was three years before he won his first honour – an FA Cup winners' medal. Since then that has been followed up with a European Cup Winners' Cup medal, a League Cup winners' medal and a league championship medal won in 1993. First capped in Scotland when he was a Celtic player in 1987 he has gone on to win more than 30 caps for his country.

McCREERY, DAVID. In five seasons McCreery managed only 57 full games for United but came on as substitute on 51 occasions. Not surprisingly he was known as 'supersub'. Irish-born McCreery was a product of United's youth system, making his debut in October 1974 as United began

Brian McClair

their assault on the second division championship. Though he was essentially a midfielder he was often obliged to fit in where necessary. He left United in August 1979, teaming up again with Tommy Docherty at QPR, and later had spells with Newcastle and in America. He was capped 23 times by Northern Ireland while he was at United but went on to win a total of 63 caps for his country.

McGLEN, BILL. Came to United at the age of 25, joining them in 1946 from Blyth Spartans. He remained at United for six seasons, six of the best in the club's history when they finished as runners up on four occasions before finally climbing to the top spot in 1952. Unfortunately McGlen only made two appearances in that season and immediately afterwards quit the club to join Lincoln City. He also missed out on United's FA Cup triumph but did total 122 games for the club. His earlier games were played at left-back but he moved to left-half to make way for John Aston. He later had a spell with Oldham.

McGRATH, PAUL. Once described as United's assassin in the middle of the field. McGrath was a hard man, a tough tackler and a dedicated ball winner for United. He came to Old Trafford from Irish football, signed from St Patrick's Athletic in March 1982, and spent seven years with the club. During much of his time at Old Trafford he was plagued by injury, perhaps an indication of the way he played, and in only one season managed to play more than half the matches. He won an FA Cup winners' medal in 1985 against Everton but then in 1989 moved to Aston Villa for £400,000 just as United were about to scoop up every honour in domestic football. His new surroundings at Villa Park seemed to agree with him, however, and he was soon the fulcrum around which an impressive Villa side was operating. McGrath played almost 200 games for United. First capped by the Republic of Ireland in 1985, he went on to pick up 31 caps while he was with United. He now has in excess of 55 caps.

McGUINNESS, WILF. United player and manager. He was a fine young United player who unfortunately is remembered more for his dismal spell as manager than for his playing career. Manchester-born McGuinness was a Busby Babe, one of many youngsters developed by the club's youth policy in the early 1950s. He appeared in three FA Youth Cup finals and also captained the England Youth team. He had joined the club as a 16-year-old and made his league debut against Wolves in October 1955. He played twice more that season as United lifted the championship and then made 13 appearances the following season as United clinched a second successive title. McGuinness did not appear in the Cup final side, however, but played a few more games as the fateful 1957–58 season kicked off. He did not make the trip to Belgrade as he was recovering from a cartilage operation but stepped into the side again later that season after the Munich disaster. He then became a regular only to have tragedy strike yet again when he broke a leg during a Central League game in December 1959. He never played again; he was still only 22 years of age. But United were generous and, realising that he still had much to offer, gave him a coaching job. The FA later appointed him as trainer of the England Youth team and during the 1966 World Cup finals Alf Ramsey used him as a training assistant. Then in April 1969 he was sensationally chosen as Busby's successor. It was an enormous job for a man who was still only 31 years old and although McGuinness oozed confidence and maturity he was to be burdened with the problem of George Best and an ageing side. Prior to his appointment United had won every trophy imaginable and it was expected that McGuinness would continue the flow. But Law, Stiles and Crerand were already past their best days while Charlton wielded his own authority and Best was frequently AWOL. The trophies failed to materialise and rifts began to emerge. In December 1970 the board stepped in, with McGuinness returning to his old job as coach and Busby taking over briefly until a new appointment was made. McGuinness later had spells managing in Greece and with York City.

McILROY, SAMMY. Popular young player of the 1970s. McIlroy joined the club in 1969 and two years later made his debut in the local derby at Maine Road. Yet despite a 63,000 crowd McIlroy showed considerable maturity and even scored. He made a few more appearances over the next couple of seasons but did not really establish himself until the 1973–74 season as United plunged into the second division. He then went on to make almost 400 appearances for the club, scoring 71 goals. McIlroy was a midfielder, full of energy and attacking purpose whose inspiration was important as United clinched the second division championship. He played in the 1976 FA Cup final and won a winners' medal the following year. Two years later he made a third appearance only to finish up a loser again. In February 1982 he signed for Stoke for £350,000 but after a discouraging time in the Potteries he returned to Manchester, this time joining City. McIlroy won his first cap for Northern Ireland in 1972 against Spain and went on to play 88 games for his country, winning 52 of these while he was a United player. It made him the most capped Northern Ireland international in United's history. McIlroy is a holder of the MBE.

McKAY, BILL. Joined United in March 1934 as the club looked destined to drop into the third division-north. He was one of four players signed to help ward off relegation. Fortunately they were successful. Scottish-born McKay had previously played with Hamilton Academicals and Bolton Wanderers. He remained with United for many years, playing 184 games and helping them back into the first division and even playing wartime football. At the end of the war he joined Stalybridge Celtic.

McLACHLAN, GEORGE. Although he was a Scot, George McLachlan had been a member of Cardiff City's FA Cup winning side in 1927. Two years after that triumph he joined United and went on to play 116 games over the next four seasons. He was a winger but the goals were rare and these were sad days for United. He managed only four in all his appearances and eventually dropped into the lower divisions with Chester.

McLENAHAN, HUGH. Versatile player of the 1920s and 30s. Manchester-born McLenahan came to the club from Stockport County in 1927 and soon stepped into the first team. Yet despite all the years he spent at Old Trafford, he was never an automatic choice and in nine seasons made just 116 appearances. Admittedly he suffered injuries in his time but his principal value to the club was as a utility player. In December 1936 he joined Notts County.

McPHERSON, FRANK. Barrow-born outside-left of the 1920s. McPherson joined United from Barrow in the summer of 1923 and soon became a regular choice. He helped United to promotion in 1925 and then scored 20 goals in his first season in first division football. He left United in 1928 after playing 175 games and scoring 52 goals to join Manchester Central and later played with Watford and Reading.

McQUEEN, GORDON. Came to United in a famous double swoop that also brought Joe Jordan to Old Trafford. Jordan had signed for United at the end of 1977, then a few weeks later Gordon McQueen joined him in a deal that cost United just under £500,000. A strong, towering centre-half he was to become the mainstay of the United defence over the next eight seasons. McQueen had been born in Ayrshire, joining Leeds from St Mirren. He was Jackie Charlton's obvious replacement and went on to win a championship medal with the Yorkshire club. He played 228 games for Manchester United, missing out only in the 1980–81 season when injury limited his appearances. McQueen liked nothing more than to try his luck in the penalty area, particularly for free kicks where his 6ft 3ins height was of obvious benefit, resulting in many of his 26 goals for the club. He played in the 1979 FA Cup final defeat by Arsenal and the 1983 League Cup final against Liverpool but finally won a winners' medal against Brighton in the 1983 FA Cup final replay, having also played in the earlier game. McQueen was already a tested Scottish international when he arrived at Old Trafford but added a further 13 caps to his collection to give him a total of 30 caps.

MANLEY, TOM. United winger of the inter-war period. Manley signed for United in 1931 and went on to make almost 200 appearances for the club, scoring 41 goals. He was unfortunate to be playing for United during their worst years but at least he was the man who saved United from the drop into the third division when he scored against Millwall in United's final game of the season. A couple of seasons later he was clutching a second division championship medal. He left United shortly before the outbreak of war to join Brentford. He played some wartime football for United but after the war returned to Brentford.

MANAGER. In a 100-year history, Manchester United Football Club have had only 16 managers. Since the war only seven men have held what is regarded as the most prestigious post in British soccer. They have been as follows:
1900–12 Ernest Mangnall
1914–21 John Robson
1921–26 John Chapman
1926–27 Clarence Hilditch
1927–31 Herbert Bamlett
1931–32 Walter Crickmer
1932–37 Scott Duncan
1938–44 Jimmy Porter
1944–45 Walter Crickmer
1945–69 Matt Busby
1969–70 Wilf McGuinness

1971–72 Frank O'Farrell
1972–77 Tommy Docherty
1977–81 Dave Sexton
1981–86 Ron Atkinson
1986– Alex Ferguson

MANAGER – LONGEST SERVING. Matt Busby holds the record as the longest-serving manager for one club in the Football League. He was manager of United for 26 seasons from October 1945 to June 1971.

MANAGER OF THE YEAR. Although a number of United managers have won the award for Manager of the Month, only one has ever claimed the honour of Manager of the Year and that was in 1993 when Alex Ferguson won the prize after lifting the league championship.

MANN, FRANK. Frank Mann looked to be nearing the end of what had been a distinguished career with Huddersfield Town when he signed for United in 1923. He was 32 years of age but astonishingly went on to play for another eight seasons. By then he was 40 and one of the oldest players to ever play for United. At Huddersfield, Mann had won an FA Cup winners' medal, starring in one of the finest teams in pre-war soccer. Had he remained at Leeds Road, however, he might have won three league championship medals. As it was, he failed to win anything at Old Trafford except promotion from the second division. Mann was what the modern game would call a midfielder, linking between defence and attack. He finally left Old Trafford in November 1929 just after United had been thrashed 2–7 by Sheffield Wednesday and joined non-league Mossley. He had played almost 200 games for United but scored only five goals.

MARKSMEN, LEAGUE. United's top league goalscorer is Bobby Charlton who struck 199 league goals during his years at Old Trafford.

125

1. Bobby Charlton 199
2. Jack Rowley 182
3. Denis Law 171
4. Dennis Viollet 159
5. Joe Spence 158
6. George Best 137

MARKSMEN, OVERALL. United's top overall marksman
is Bobby Charlton whose total of 247 goals for the club
looks safe for many years to come.
1. Bobby Charlton 247
2. Denis Law 236
3. Jack Rowley 208
4. Dennis Viollet 178
5. George Best 178
6. Joe Spence 168
7. Stan Pearson 149
8. David Herd 144
9. Tommy Taylor 128

MELLOR, JOHN. Full-back signed from non-league Wit-
ton Albion in 1930. Mellor made his debut in September
1930 and was a regular choice for the next three seasons.
However, he made only eight appearances in his final three
seasons with the club and left to join Cardiff City in 1937 as
United were relegated. He played a total of 122 games for
the club.

MEREDITH, BILLY. One of the greatest names in the
history of Manchester United Football Club and the most
outstanding player of his era. Without Meredith United
would undoubtedly never have won two league championships and the FA Cup in the period before the First World
War. It was Meredith who put United on the footballing
map, helping to lay the foundations that have made it such
a famous club today. He came to United in 1906, already a
Cup winner with Manchester City. His transfer from City
caused a sensation, following a scandal that had led to his

being banned from playing for City. A former coalminer, Meredith made his debut for United on New Year's Day 1907, just a few days after his transfer from City. By the end of the following season United were champions. Meredith was a right-winger but never a goalscorer. In his entire United career of 332 matches he only managed 35 goals. But that hardly tells the full tale. Meredith was a wizard, a man who could dribble the ball down the length of the touchline and then fling over an inch-perfect cross for Sandy Turnbull though he was equally adept at cutting inside and working his way into the penalty area. And as always there would be the unmistakable toothpick gripped between his teeth as he worked his way down the flanks. He was born in Chirk in North Wales and signed on as an amateur with City in 1894. He was already a legend by the time he came to United with 339 appearances and 146 goals. After winning the league championship for United Meredith then helped them to the FA Cup the following season and two years later to a second championship. In between he also helped cause a strike as the players' union, which he had helped form, went into dispute with the Football Association. Meredith was a renegade; he did things his way and if the authorities did not like it, then it was their hard luck. Above all he believed passionately in the rights of players and throughout his career stood for the freedom of players to move from club to club and to be paid a decent wage. It frequently got him into trouble and on more than one occasion he was accused of bribing opponents. Meredith officially remained with United until after the First World War although during the war he had guested with City. Then, in August 1921 he decided to take on a new role with his old club Manchester City as coach and player. He was capped 48 times by Wales, scoring 11 goals for his country, making his first appearance in 1895 and his final appearance in 1920 to give him one of the longest international careers in history. His playing career in the Football league was just as long, stretching from 1894 until March 1924 when he appeared in an FA Cup semi-final in his fiftieth year.

MEW, JOHN. Goalkeeper John Mew played with United for 14 seasons, making 199 appearances. Born in Sunderland, he came to United in October 1912, making his first appearance a year later. He played only a handful of games before war broke out but came into his own during the war, playing many games for United. In the years after the war he was first choice and went on to win an England cap in 1921. He also played in the 1920 match for England against South Africa. He was said to be on the small side for a goalkeeper but nobody at Old Trafford ever had any complaints about his ability. He left United in September 1926 to join Barrow and later had coaching spells in Belgium and South America.

MILK CUP. See Football League Cup.

MILLER, TOM. Centre-forward of the Edwardian era who came from a large footballing family. His brother John was also a footballer who played with Liverpool while four of his cousins appeared for Hamilton Academicals. Tom himself had played for the Accies before joining Liverpool in February 1912. Over the next eight years he made 146 appearances, scoring 58 goals for Liverpool although his career was badly interrupted by the First World War. He appeared in the 1914 Cup final for Liverpool and was one of a number of players suspended by the FA after being involved in the rigging of a game against Manchester United on Good Friday 1915. Ironically, Miller left Liverpool in 1920 to join, of all clubs, Manchester United. He had just one season at Old Trafford, playing 27 games and scoring eight goals. He was capped three times for Scotland, once while he was with Liverpool and twice in his season at United.

MILLION-POUND PLAYER. United's first million-pound player was Garry Birtles, signed from Nottingham

Forest for £1.25 million in October 1980. It was a signing that turned out to be a disaster. Birtles was at Old Trafford for just one year, scoring a mere 12 goals in 64 appearances. He was then resold to Forest for £300,000.

MITTEN, CHARLIE. Will always be remembered for his part in what was to become known as the 'Bogota affair'. Mitten was an outstanding player who had joined the club in 1936 but had to wait until after the war before making his league debut. During the war he guested with various clubs including Tranmere Rovers and Aston Villa and it soon became apparent that he was an unusually talented player. After the war he went straight into the United side and was always first choice. Mitten played on the left wing but he could also score goals. He had a stunning shot and in March 1950 he scored three penalties as United thrashed Aston Villa 7–0. He in fact scored four goals that day. Ironically, they were to be the last he would ever score for the club because in June of that year Mitten, along with a number of other leading professionals, quit the English game and signed for the Colombian side Sante Fe. Mitten was promised huge sums of money, much of which never appeared, and he was soon on the plane back home. But his sudden disappearance had angered United, and especially manager Matt Busby, who had always rated him one of the most outstanding players the club had ever known. Nor had United been given any transfer money and although Mitten wanted to come back to Old Trafford, Busby was unforgiving. Mitten was immediately placed on the transfer list, eventually joining Fulham. His career was never quite the same after that although he enjoyed a few seasons at Craven Cottage and later played with Mansfield. He then went into management, having a successful spell with Newcastle United. He played 161 games for United, scoring 61 goals, and won a Cup winners' medal in 1948 but was surprisingly never capped by England.

MOGER, HARRY. Goalkeeper to the famous United side

that won so many honours during the Edwardian era. Moger came to United from Southern League Southampton in 1903 and went staight into the United line-up. After that he was rarely absent, playing 264 games over the next nine seasons. During that time he claimed two league championship medals and starred in the FA Cup final against Bristol City. Tall and lean, Moger was said to be effective in high-ball situations. He liked to come off his line and punch the ball clear and was one of the first exponents of this tactic. He retired in 1912 but was never capped by England.

MOORE, CHARLIE. Only a few players in the club's history have played more league games than Charlie Moore. And yet, despite 328 appearances, Moore never managed to score for United. He was born in Staffordshire and came to Old Trafford in May 1919, straight from non-league football. Moore was a full-back, highly regarded and as safe as they come. When Moore was around United played with confidence; when he was absent they were jittery. He missed the entire 1921–22 season through injury and not surprisingly United were relegated.

MORAN, KEVIN. Has the dubious honour of being the first player ever to be sent off in an FA Cup final when he up-ended Everton's Peter Reid with a rather clumsy tackle. If anything, however, the referee's somewhat excessive action only spurred United on to win a 1–0 win over the Mersey-siders. It meant that Moran was not officially eligible for a medal but after an appeal by the club, the FA relented. It was Moran's second medal, having already picked one up in the 1983 final against Brighton. He signed for United from the Irish club Pegasus in February 1978 and made his debut a year later. But it was not until the 1980–81 season that he secured his place and from then on was only ever out of the side because of injury though he did experience more than his fair share of injuries. Moran was the bite in the centre of the United defence, as tough a tackler as any in the Football

League. It may have won him few friends outside of Old Trafford but it certainly saved United on many an occasion. He won his first international honour with Eire in 1980 when he played against Switzerland and ten years later appeared with the Irish in the 1990 World Cup finals. He won 38 caps for Eire while he was with United, a record for the club, and has now picked up more than 60 caps for his country. After almost 300 games with United he left during the 1988 close season to join Sporting Gijon in the Spanish League. He returned to England in 1990 to join Blackburn Rovers.

MORGAN, WILLIE. Skilful Scottish winger and midfielder who epitomised the United style of the late 1960s and early 70s. Born in Alloa, Morgan came to United from Burnley as a £110,000 signing in 1968. He quickly settled into the side and was an ever present for most of his Old Trafford career, making almost 300 appearances. He began as a winger but was later shifted into the midfield where he proved to be even more effective. He scored 33 times for United although his contribution was more in laying on goals than finding the net himself. He left United during the summer of 1975 to rejoin Burnley and a short time later signed for Bolton where his career was revived as the team clinched promotion to the first division. In 1978 he was involved in a messy court action when his former manager Tommy Docherty instigated proceedings against him and Granada Television. Morgan won his first Scottish cap in 1968 with Burnley and then won 20 more caps while he was a United player.

MORRIS, JOHNNY. Post-war inside-forward who won a Cup winners' medal with United. He joined United just one month before war broke out but had to wait seven years before making his league debut in the 0–3 defeat by Sunderland. It might have lost him his place but Busby kept faith in him and he was virtually ever present for the rest of his Old Trafford career. In his second season he scored 21

131

goals, and laid on Jack Rowley's goal which helped turn the Cup final United's way. Morris had considerable style and was always a handful for any defender. He could dribble, turn and pass with some style but was also something of an individualist who was always likely to question the manager's tactics. Unfortunately, he did it once too often, and Busby promptly transfer-listed him. It was a surprising move and it was not long before Derby County had snapped him up, paying a British record fee of £24,500 in March 1949. Morris's career at the Baseball Ground proved to be just as successful with three England caps and three games for the Football League. In October 1952 he left Derby and joined Leicester City, twice helping them to the second division championship. He played a total of 92 games for United, scoring 35 goals.

MOSES, REMI. One of Ron Atkinson's signings for United in a double swoop on his former club West Bromwich Albion that took Moses and Bryan Robson to Old Trafford. That was in October 1981 and the 20-year-old Moses cost United £600,000. Born in Manchester he had been a lifelong United supporter and jumped at the chance to return home. A strong, aggressive midfielder, Moses did not always enjoy the best of luck at Old Trafford. Injury cut into his career, limiting his appearances, and in 1990 he decided to retire. He had only played 150 league games for the club, but when he did play Moses was a force to be reckoned with, his bone-crunching tackles halting attackers in their stride and bringing the kind of authority to the United midfield that every team needs if it is to succeed.

MUHREN, ARNOLD. Dutch international who brought a touch of class and elegance to the United midfield during the 1980s. Muhren came to United from Ipswich after earlier playing in Holland with Ajax and Twente Enschende. At Ajax he had twice been substitute for European Cup finals though he never actually came on. He did, however, collect a UEFA Cup winners' medal with

Remi Moses

Ipswich. He arrived at Old Trafford in 1982 and went on to play almost 100 games for United, scoring 18 goals, but after three seasons injury began to dog his career and he soon lost his place. In June 1985 he grabbed an opportunity to return to Dutch football, signing for his former club Ajax.

MUNICH. On Thursday 6 February 1958 the Manchester United team travelling back from a European Cup quarter-final game against Red Star Belgrade was involved in a plane crash at Munich Airport. The plane, a BEA Eliz-abethan Airliner, had stopped to refuel at Munich. With the weather deteriorating in a snowstorm the plane made three attempts to take off but on the third attempt it failed to gain any height and crashed at the end of the runway. Twenty-one people were killed instantly. Two others, including the United player Duncan Edwards, would later add to the toll. Eight United players were among the final victims. They were: Roger Byrne, Tommy Taylor, Duncan Edwards, Eddie Colman, Mark Jones, Bill Whelan, Geoff Bent and David Pegg. The United coach and former player Bert Whalley and trainer Tom Curry were also killed, along with the United secretary Walter Crickmer. Matt Busby was seriously injured and spent many weeks in hospital. Eight journalists were also killed including Frank Swift, the former Manchester City and England goalkeeper. Two crew members also died along with two passengers. Although Johnny Berry and Jackie Blanchflower survived they never played football again.

MURPHY, JIMMY. Assistant manager of United under Busby who took over as temporary manager following the Munich air disaster. Murphy played most of his football with West Brom, winning 15 Welsh caps before the outbreak of war. During the war he met Matt Busby and when Busby was appointed manager at Old Trafford he immediately recruited Murphy as his assistant, although he was not officially called assistant manager until 1955.

During the 1950s Murphy was also manager of Wales and was said to have been offered jobs managing Brazil, Juventus and Arsenal. But instead he chose to stay at Old Trafford, remaining loyal to the club for the rest of his life. International duty with Wales meant that Murphy missed the trip to Belgrade for the European game against Red Star. After the disaster it was Murphy who had to take over, sign players and mentally prepare everyone to continue. It was an extraordinary task and that United did not immediately fold was due almost entirely to his endeavours. His own desperate thoughts were shunted aside so that when Busby returned he found a club still thriving and just as determined as ever. Many regard Murphy as the inspiration behind United's youth policy and it was certainly Murphy who dealt with the youngsters on a day-to-day basis. He remained with the club until 1971 when he retired. Sadly there was some bitterness with Murphy feeling that he still had much to offer and that his views were being ignored.

MUTCH, GEORGE. Scottish international who is probably best remembered for his last-minute penalty that won the FA Cup for Preston in 1938. Mutch joined United from Arbroath, an £800 signing, in May 1934. United had avoided relegation by a whisker the previous season and were in desperate need of a goalscorer. Mutch was the solution and very effective he was too. He netted 19 goals in his first season and 23 in his second as United won promotion. The goals dried up the following year as United slid out of the first division and early into the 1937–38 campaign United sold him to Preston. The Lancashire club were to be very grateful, especially as six months later he slotted Preston's penalty into the back of the net to win the FA Cup with the only goal of the game. After the war he had a brief spell with Bury and Southport. Mutch was capped just once by Scotland, while he was with Preston.

N

NEWTON HEATH. When United were formed in 1878 they were known as Newton Heath. They had been founded by a group of railway workers employed at the carriage and wagon department of the Lancashire and Yorkshire railways at the Newton Heath depot. They originally adopted the name Newton Heath (LYR) but dropped the initials LYR as the club became more popular and expanded its activities, recruiting players from outside the local railway yard. They kept the name Newton Heath until 1902 when, following the club's bankruptcy, they changed their name to Manchester United.

NICHOLL, JIMMY. Perhaps the only Canadian-born player to ever turn out for Manchester United. Although he had been born across the Atlantic, Nicholl's family had returned to England and Nicholl began his Old Trafford career while still a teenager, turning professional in 1974. Even more unusual, he then went on to play for Northern Ireland. He made his United debut that same season, substituting for Martin Buchan in the 1–0 win at Southampton. The following season proved to be even more satisfying with 18 appearances plus seven more as substitute as he stood in for the injured Alex Forsyth. By the beginning of the 1976–77 campaign Nicholl had laid claim to Forsyth's jersey and was to be a permanent fixture over the next five seasons. A forceful, athletic defender he could also show a turn of pace. He won a winners' medal in the 1977 FA Cup final against Liverpool but was on the losing side two years later against Arsenal. In all he appeared 234/13 times for United, scoring six goals. His career came to an abrupt end in 1981 with the signing of John Gidman and he was loaned out to Sunderland before returning to Canada to play with Toronto Blizzards. He later had spells with Sunderland again, Glasgow Rangers and West Brom. He was capped at all levels for Northern Ireland, winning an impressive 73 full caps for his country of adoption, 41 of these coming while he was at Old Trafford. He also appeared in two World Cup finals.

NICKNAME. United's nickname for many years has been either 'United' or the 'Red Devils'.

NORTH ROAD. The first ever home of the club when it was still known as Newton Heath. North Road, off Monsall Road in Newton Heath, was on the edge of a clay pit and the changing-rooms were half a mile down the road at the Three Crowns public house. The pitch was also reputed to be appalling and was renowned as a mud bath. The club left North Road in September 1893 and moved across the city to Bank Street.

O

O'FARRELL, FRANK. United manager, 1971–72. Frank O'Farrell arrived at Old Trafford as the perfect solution to the club's continuing problems following the retirement of Matt Busby. He was older and far more experienced in management than Busby's immediate successor Wilf McGuinness. What's more he had a proven track record, having steered an attractive Leicester City side to the second division championship as well as guiding Torquay from the fourth to the third division. And as if to show their full confidence in their new man, United promoted Busby out of the way and on to the board. Even George Best welcomed his appointment although his approval would not last long. O'Farrell was a shrewd, genial Irishman, a former West Ham and Preston half-back and Irish international who seemed more than capable of sorting out the dressing-room rows of Old Trafford. But during his short reign he was to encounter the same problem again and again – George Best. The gifted Irishman was in decline, always likely to go AWOL, and just as unreliable on the field as off it. O'Farrell tried all means of coaxing Best. He befriended him, he encouraged him, he excused him, then he dropped him and finally, his patience snapping, he placed him on the transfer list only to find that Best and Busby were secretly meeting to iron out the problems. Best's name was taken off the list and with that act O'Farrell's authority was usurped. It was the beginning of the end. United had begun well under O'Farrell, leaping to the top of the table in his first season in charge, but had then fallen away as the dressing-room tiffs continued. The next season they went into rapid decline and when they were thrashed 0–5 at Crystal Palace the writing was on the wall. Even before half-time Busby was alleged to have been chatting with Tommy Docherty. And so in December 1972 O'Farrell was sacked with three-and-a-half years of his contract still to run. Ironically, George Best was also given his marching orders the same day. O'Farrell's problem had undoubtedly been George Best all along but he had failed to resolve the difficulty at an early stage when he still had the confidence of the board and players. Though whether the public would ever have allowed Best to be transferred at that point is another matter. When he did finally take steps the United board failed to back him. But there were others who felt that O'Farrell was aloof and not a team man. Denis Law complained that they never saw him, that he was a stranger to them. O'Farrell's third problem was in the transfer market. He had failed to realise the desperate need for a midfielder and a centre-half and although players were available he had failed to take the plunge and had instead become obsessed with finding a striker. During his stay O'Farrell made only a handful of forays into the transfer market and most were unsuccessful. Only Martin Buchan made the grade. Less exciting were Ted MacDougall, a £200,000 striker from third division Bournemouth, Wyn Davies, another striker who failed to find the net, and Ian Storey-Moore whose promising career was cut short by injury. If only finding a striker had been O'Farrell's biggest worry he might have survived many more years at Old Trafford. As it was, he was given too little time and not enough authority.

OLD TRAFFORD. Home of Manchester United since February 1910. United's previous grounds at North Road and Bank Street had both been appalling and following the league title win in 1908 and their FA Cup victory in 1909 the club decided on a move to a new stadium, especially built for them, and that would match their footballing triumphs. The stadium was designed by Archibald Leitch, the noted architect of many football grounds. It was originally designed to be the biggest ground in the country, capable of holding 100,000 spectators with the plushest of facilities for players and staff. The site was purchased with a £60,000 grant from the chairman John Davies but with construction costs at an extra £30,000, some of the planned facilities had to be scaled down. Instead of holding 100,000, the capacity was reduced to 70,000 and some of the office facilities, including the billiard room, had to be scrapped. But it was still a magnificent stadium. It was opened on Saturday 19 February 1910 with Liverpool as the visitors. The gate was reckoned to be about 50,000 although a few thousand more were said to have sneaked in free of charge

Old Trafford

when gatemen, unable to cope with the queues, simply opened the doors. Old Trafford's biggest attendance came many years later when 76,962 watched the FA Cup semi-final between Wolves and Grimsby in March 1939. In 1915 Old Trafford hosted the FA Cup final between Sheffield United and Chelsea and in 1911 and 1970 it staged Cup final replays. In 1966 it was chosen as a venue for the World Cup finals. Over the years Old Trafford has hosted several internationals and inter-league games. In 1992 the famous Stretford End was pulled down as the club began a massive redevelopment that would turn Old Trafford into an all-seater stadium. Often called the 'theatre of dreams', Old Trafford is today capable of holding 44,000 spectators. And with its executive boxes and banqueting facilities, it is probably the finest stadium in the country.

Old Trafford

OLIVE, LES. Although Les Olive played just two games for United, both in the league, he was to enjoy many successful years as the club's secretary. He joined the groundstaff in 1942 when he was still only 14 years old, working in the office as well as playing for the reserves and juniors. His big opportunity came in April 1953 when goalkeepers Ray Wood, Jack Crompton and Reg Allen were all injured. Although Olive was more of an outfield player than a goalkeeper, he was the best United could offer and in the emergency had to don the goalkeeper's jersey. He was not altogether unsuccessful either. United won their first game 2–1 at Newcastle and then drew 2–2 at Old Trafford with West Brom. And that was it. He never played first-team football again although he continued to turn out for the reserves. By the time of the Munich disaster he had worked his way up to assistant secretary and when the club secretary Walter Crickmer was killed at Munich, Les Olive took over the reigns. It was a position he was to hold for many years. He is now a club director.

OLSEN, JESPER. Danish international Jesper Olsen was signed from the famous Dutch club Ajax in July 1984 for a

Jesper Olsen

fee of £800,000. He was a typical winger, small, wiry and fast, whose skill could at times be breathtaking. He had begun his footballing career with the Danish club Naestved before joining Ajax in 1981. Although he had a useful career at Old Trafford, Olsen was always inclined to drift in and out of matches. When United were winning he could be glorious but when they were losing, his head would drop. But he was always a Ron Atkinson favourite, underlining Atkinson's commitment to daring, adventurous football. Once Atkinson had gone, Olsen's days were numbered and it was not long before new manager Alex Ferguson had dispensed with his services, selling him to Bordeaux. He made just over 150 appearances for United, scoring 24 goals, and played 25 games for Denmark while he was with United.

OLYMPICS. You would not expect a United player to be associated with the Olympic games yet in Harold Hardman, United had not just an Olympic footballer, but a gold medal winner as well. Hardman, who joined United from Everton in 1908, won a gold medal that same year with the Great Britain soccer side. He qualified for the Great Britain Olympic team because he was an amateur. Yet he also won four full England caps. After playing for United he became a director of the club and was for many years its chairman.

OUTCASTS. The name given to the group of United players in 1909 who refused to denounce the trade union they had helped form. Two of United's most famous names, Billy Meredith and Charlie Roberts, were among those behind the union but the footballing authorities did not take kindly to the idea, and in 1909 a new ruling effectively banned the new Players' Union and players were forced to sign a new contract denouncing it. One by one players in all the major clubs duly signed but the United players held out, refusing point blank to give their support to the club. In the end United banned their entire Cup winning side of three months earlier for refusing to sign. But the United players stood firm and went off to Fallowfield on their own to train for the forthcoming season. A special team photograph was taken and Charlie Roberts chalked the name 'outcasts' on a blackboard. The name stuck. Then, unexpectedly, the outcasts started to gain support from other clubs. Both the Everton and Liverpool players changed their minds and suddenly it looked as if the new season would not be able to get underway. There were frantic discussions and in the end a compromise was reached. But thanks to the resilience of the United players, a trade union had been born which would go on to flourish.

OVERSEAS PLAYERS. Prior to the 1980s United's overseas players had mostly been South Africans but in 1980 they added a new dimension to their collection with the signing of the Yugoslav Nikola Jovanovic. Two years later they signed the Dutch midfielder Arnold Muhren. They were to be the first of a number of continental players who joined the club over the next few years. They have included the Danes Jesper Olsen, Johnny Sivebaek and Peter Schmeichel, the Ukrainian Andrei Kanchelskis and the Frenchman Eric Cantona.

P

PALLISTER, GARY. When Gary Pallister joined United from Middlesbrough in 1989 it was for a record British fee of £2.4 million. Pallister had come to prominence in Middlesbrough's promotion race from the second division and had already received the call from the then England manager Bobby Robson. But it was a hefty gamble by Alex Ferguson for a 24-year-old who still had much to prove. A towering 6ft 4ins defender, Pallister did not always look comfortable in his first season at Old Trafford but as time progressed he began to look more confident and sure and by 1992 was impressing his colleagues enough to be named PFA Player of the Year. He had also collected a few more England caps as well as an FA Cup winners' medal and a League Cup winners' medal. Then in 1993 he won a league championship medal and was generally regarded as one of the main reasons why United conceded only 31 goals. Still only 27 years of age, Pallister looks destined to spend many more years at the heart of the United defence and to collect a few more England caps as well.

PAPE, ALBERT. The subject of one of the most bizarre transfer deals in United's history. Pape was due to be

Gary Pallister

playing for Clapton Orient against United at Old Trafford in a second division fixture in February 1925 but shortly before the kick off the two clubs agreed the transfer of Pape to United. The deal was cleared with the FA on the telephone and Pape, instead of pulling on Orient's colours for the afternoon, strolled across the corridor to the United dressing-room and pulled on a United shirt. He had been listed in the programme at centre-forward for Orient and much to the surprise of the crowd he was suddenly announced to be playing in that role for United. At the time it seemed a canny deal as Pape scored to help United to a 4–2 win but he did not last long at Old Trafford, playing just 18 games in eight months before joining Fulham.

PARKER, PAUL. Defender signed from Queens Park Rangers in the summer of 1991. Parker had begun his footballing career with Fulham where he made over 150 league appearances before joining QPR. Although he had looked promising at Fulham he really began to shine as a QPR player and had already picked up 16 England caps before United moved in with an offer that brought him to Old Trafford. A neat, constructive defender with the ability to pass the ball under pressure, he has brought a calmness and reassurance to the United defence with his elegant passing and control. He won a League Cup winners' medal as United defeated Nottingham Forest at Wembley and a championship medal in 1993. Parker is also clearly part of Graham Taylor's England plans and has continued to add international caps to his collection since joining United.

PARTRIDGE, TED. Outside-left who joined United from Ebbw Vale in 1920. He made 160 appearances for the club during the inter-war years, many in the second division. He was said to be a goalmaker rather than a goalscorer and his total of just 18 goals would appear to bear out this claim. He began his Old Trafford days as a regular but after three seasons found himself discarded and his appearances were rare until the 1927–28 season when he returned to enjoy 23 outings. The following season he left United, joining Halifax Town.

PEARSON, STAN. Post-war inside-forward with a goal-scoring instinct that was largely responsible for helping United to so many honours during the period. Born in Salford, Pearson came to Old Trafford shortly before the war and had just over 20 appearances to his name when hostilities broke out. He continued to play wartime football for United but returned after the war to become one of the most effective inside-forwards in the Football League, both scoring goals and making them for his partner Jack Rowley. It was Pearson who hit a hat-trick in the FA Cup semi-final against Derby County at Hillsborough that secured United a place in the final and it was Pearson who struck again at Wembley. That season he managed 26 goals in all competitions with eight of them coming in the FA Cup. Pearson was an outstanding inside-forward; resolute, skilled, a fine distributor of the ball and with an eye for goal. In 345 appearances he managed an impressive 149 goals and, along with Jack Rowley, scored more than half the team's goals during the side's championship season of 1951–52. Had the war not intervened, no doubt Pearson would have scored even more goals as well as winning a great many more England caps than the mere eight he won. He made his England debut in 1948 and his final appearance was against Italy in 1952. In 1954 he ended his 17-year-old association with United by signing for Bury. He later had a spell with Chester where he was also manager.

PEARSON, STUART. Highly popular striker who was signed from Hull City for £200,000 towards the end of the 1973–74 season as part of Tommy Docherty's reorganisation plans. Born in Hull, Pearson had joined Hull City as an apprentice and made 129 appearances for the club before joining United. He had a typical goalscorer's instinct and although his figures do not always look impressive on paper, to judge him in this way would be to ignore the many

opportunities he created for his colleagues, particularly Lou
Macari. Small for a striker, Pearson was nevertheless strong
and fast and was considered highly enough to collect 15
England caps. He won his first England honour against
Wales in 1976 and for the best part of two years was the
regular choice as England's target man. Pearson was always
a bubbly character, well liked by the Old Trafford crowd
and always an enthusiast. He played in both the 1976 and
1977 Cup finals, scoring in the 1977 final to help United
beat Liverpool. In 1979 Pearson left United, signing for
West Ham in a £220,000 deal and a year later was back at
Wembley as West Ham won the FA cup. In all he played
178 games for Manchester United, scoring a total of 66
goals, and enjoying his best season in 1976–77 when he
netted 19 goals.

PEDDIE, JOHN. Early Edwardian centre-forward who
enjoyed two spells with United. Glasgow-born Peddie
began his career with Third Lanark but was soon snapped
up by Newcastle where he starred for five years, scoring 62
goals in 125 games. In 1902, after an unusually barren spell,
he joined United. In his first season he scored 15 goals in 36
outings but was then surprisingly transferred to Southern
League Plymouth Argyle. A year later he was back in
Manchester where he went on to enjoy another three
seasons. In 1908 he returned to Scotland, joining Hearts in
a deal that also took Richard Wombwell and W. Yates north
of the border. In his United career Peddie scored 58 goals
in 121 appearances.

PEGG, DAVID. Outside-left who died in the Munich
disaster. Doncaster-born Pegg came to Old Trafford as a
youngster and starred in the club's 1953 Youth Cup
triumph. But even by then he had made his debut in the first
team, playing 19 games during the 1952–53 season when he
was still 17 years old. Over the next couple of seasons his
appearances were limited, however, as he made way for
more experienced colleagues. But by 1955 he had secured

the number eleven shirt and wore it with distinction over the next few seasons as United stormed to two successive league championships and an FA Cup final. Pegg was a typical left-winger, short, pacey and happy to run with the ball. He played in the famous European run of the 1956–57 season that culminated in the defeat by Real Madrid. He also played a few European games the following season although by the time of the ill-fated Red Star game he had lost his place to Albert Scanlon. Although Pegg was not in the starting line-up for the Red Star match he nevertheless made the trip to Belgrade and was tragically killed at Munich. He was capped at England Youth and Under-23 level, but won only one full England cap, starring with three of his United colleagues against the Republic of Ireland in a World Cup qualifier in 1957. Pegg had played just 148 games for United, scoring 28 goals, at the time of his death.

PENALTY SHOOT-OUTS. United have been involved in some memorable penalty shoot-outs. One of the most dramatic was the shoot-out at the end of the UEFA Cup tie with Moscow Torpedo in September 1992 which United lost.

PHELAN, MIKE. Signed from Norwich during the summer of 1989. Born in Lancashire, midfielder Phelan had played with Burnley for a number of seasons when Norwich snapped him up for a mere £45,000, and almost immediately made him team captain. He came to United in 1989 for a fee of £750,000, after rejecting offers from Everton, Spurs and Nottingham Forest. He sometimes featured as a centre-back with Norwich but is really a midfield player which is where he has enjoyed most of his United success. He won his first England cap in 1990, coming on as a substitute for Bryan Robson, but has scooped up a few honours with United including a European Cup-Winners' Cup medal, a League Cup winners' medal, an FA Cup winners' medal and a championship medal.

Michael Phelan

PICKEN, JOHN. Scottish-born, Edwardian inside-forward who kicked off his professional career with Bolton Wanderers in 1899. After Bolton, where he had proved to be particularly prolific in front of goal, he moved to Plymouth Argyle in the Southern League but joined United in 1905. In his first season he netted 25 goals in 37 outings but was never anywhere near as prolific in his remaining years with the club, scoring just 21 goals over the next five seasons. At one point he even lost his place to Sandy Turnbull and missed out on a league championship and FA Cup winners' medal. However, he was back for the 1910–11 season when United won their second championship. At the end of that season Picken moved to Burnley and later had a spell with Bristol City.

PITCH. The Old Trafford pitch measures 116 yards × 76 yards.

PROGRAMME. The United programme has been in existence since the club's foundation, going back to its days when it was known as Newton Heath. For many years it was a single sheet of paper with the team line-ups and a few assorted adverts and often with a fixture list for the season. As the game developed, however, so the programme changed. The day's fixtures were listed with space for half-time scores and a few, often inaccurate, statistics were also given, usually goalscorers and appearances. During the Edwardian age there was an editorial and perhaps a few notes about the opposition. But the United programme really came into its own after the Second World War when it adopted a style that has continued until today. The modern programme now has a highly illustrated colour format with statistics and information about the opposition as well as details about United's players and reserve team results. Since the war the front cover of the programme has carried the now famous masthead of a player and supporter shaking hands. Only the styles of kits and clothes have changed. The current editor is Cliff Butler.

PROMOTION. United have been promoted on five occasions, always from the second division to the first. They were first promoted in 1906 when they were runners up in the second division and were automatically promoted. They were next promoted in 1925 when again they finished second in division two. In 1936 they finished as champions of the second division and were promoted for a third time. Two years later they were again promoted, this time as runners up. Their fifth promotion season was 1974–75 when they won the second division title under manager Tommy Docherty.

PUBLIC COMPANY. Manchester United became a public limited company quoted on the Stock Exchange in 1991.

Q

QUIXALL, ALBERT. Albert Quixall was regarded as the golden boy of British football when he signed for United in September 1958, just six months after the Munich disaster. Tall, blond and handsome, Quixall cost United a British record fee of £45,000 from Sheffield Wednesday although he himself collected a mere £20 as his signing-on fee. Despite his youthful looks, Quixall was vastly experienced, the holder of two second division championship medals and five England caps as well as a host of Under-23 and England B honours. In almost 250 league games for his home club Sheffield Wednesday, he had netted 63 goals. After the loss of so many of their young stars United needed to replenish their ranks with some youthful, proven quality. Ernie Taylor and Stan Crowther had been signed in the aftermath of Munich but both offered short-term rather than long-term solutions. Quixall was still only 25 when he joined the club and soon proved to be a good investment. He enjoyed six seasons at Old Trafford, making 183 appearances and scoring 56 goals though he had to wait some time before he collected any honours. His only medal came in 1963 when he was a member of United's Cup winning side. Throughout his Old Trafford career he was ignored by the England selectors although he did manage an appearance for the Football League against the Scottish League in 1958. Quixall, with his dashing looks and pace, brought a touch of glamour back to United and his partnership with Charlton and Viollet upfront rekindled memories of the Busby Babes. A year after winning his only honour at Old Trafford Quixall was transferred to Oldham Athletic for £7,000. Two years later he moved to Stockport but retired from league football the following year.

Albert Quixall

R

RECORDS. Manchester United have beaten plenty of footballing records over the years and have also produced one or two recordings. Most are best forgotten but almost certainly the pick of the bunch is *Glory, Glory, Man United* released for the 1983 FA Cup final. Another memorable record, this time one about a United player, was *Georgie Best, the Belfast Boy.*

REDWOOD, HUBERT. A fine defender who like so many players found his career interrupted by war just as he was reaching his peak. Redwood, from St Helens, joined United, his first professional club, at the comparatively old age of 22. A year later he was lining up in the first team in a goalless draw with Tottenham. It was, by all accounts, a none too impressive start and he had to wait another 12 months before donning a United shirt again. This time he proved his worth and became a regular until war broke out. He continued to play wartime football while serving in the army but contracted tuberculosis and died in 1943 at the age of 30. He had played 96 games for United, scoring four goals.

REFEREES. United once had a manager who had been a Football League referee. He was Herbert Bamlett who was manager at Old Trafford between 1927 and 1931. Earlier in his life Bamlett had refereed the 1915 FA Cup final between Burnley and Liverpool at the Crystal Palace. Not only was he the youngest man to ever referee a Cup final but it was also the first Cup final to be played in front of a reigning monarch, King George V. Bamlett was also the referee for the United–Burnley FA Cup quarter-final game played at Turf Moor in 1909. With United losing 0–1 and with just 18 minutes remaining, Bamlett controversially abandoned the game in deteriorating weather. In the replayed match United won and went on to lift the FA Cup. J. J. Bentley, for many years a chairman and secretary of the club, was also a Football League referee for some years before he came to United.

REID, TOM. Although Tom Reid played more than 50 games for Liverpool he found far greater fame with Manchester United. Yet it was surprising that Liverpool should ever have let him go, especially as he had scored 31 goals in his 51 league appearances. They were impressive figures and they continued at Old Trafford with Reid knocking in 67 goals in 107 outings, though they were still not enough to stop United sliding into the second division. Eighteen months later he was on the move again, this time to Oldham where his prolific goalscoring continued unabated. Reid had joined Liverpool in 1926 from Clydebank and signed for United in 1929.

RELEGATION. United have been relegated only five times and always from the first to the second division. Their first taste of it came in 1894 after just two seasons in the first division. Unfortunately they had to wait until 1906 before they returned to the upper division. They were next relegated in 1921, and again in 1931. In 1937 they had another taste of relegation after just one season back in the first division but did not suffer the humiliation again until 1974.

REST OF EUROPE. Three United players have played for the Rest of Europe in various international matches. The first was Johnny Carey who played against Great Britain at Hampden Park in May 1947. Both Bobby Charlton and Denis Law have also represented Europe with both turning out against Scandinavia in 1964.

REST OF THE WORLD. Denis Law is the only United player to have ever been chosen to play for the Rest of the World when he played against England at Wembley in 1963.

ROBERTS, CHARLIE. One of the great names in the club's early history. Roberts was for many years captain of United, inspiring them to two league championships and the FA Cup during their first ever run of glory. Born in Darlington, Roberts first starred with Bishop Auckland before he joined Grimsby Town but after just one season with Grimsby he was snapped up by the United manager Ernest Mangall in April 1904 for £400. It was to be the beginning of a golden era for United. Roberts was to spend ten seasons with them, making 299 appearances, and scoring 23 goals. He was the backbone of a fine United side. A centre-half who was not only bold and combative but above all a footballer. He was also fast and was said to be able to run the 100 yards in 11 seconds when the world record stood at 9.6 seconds. The great Italian manager Vitorio Pozzo, who was a regular visitor to United when he lived in England, even fashioned his World Cup winning side of 1934 around the style of Charlie Roberts. The United manager Ernest Mangnall gave Roberts the freedom to play as he wished and he responded with confidence and responsibility. Yet Roberts was not always the easiest of characters; he was his own man. He was a founding member and a leading light of the players' trade union and one of the most determined when the United players came out on strike in 1909. He was also one of the first players to wear his shorts above his thighs when everyone else had them dangling around their knees, something which regularly brought him into trouble with the authorities. All this perhaps helps explain why such an outstanding player was only capped three times by England, although it is a poor excuse for the selectors. Roberts led his life as he did on the football pitch, with dignity and principle. Under his captaincy United won two league championships and the FA Cup but then shortly after his mentor Mangnall had left Old Trafford, Roberts too departed, joining Oldham Athletic in August 1913. It was to be United's loss as they slumped into the relegation zone while Oldham almost clinched the title. The outbreak of war marked an inevitable end to Roberts's playing career although he was later tempted out of retirement to manage Oldham. It was to be a job he found unusually stressful, however, and after just 18 months he quit and returned to the peace and quiet of his newsagent's shop.

ROBINS, MARK. Young United striker who failed to make the grade and was sold to Norwich during the summer of 1992. United's loss, however, proved to be Norwich's gain as Robins hit 15 goals in his first season, helping the unfancied East Anglian club into third spot. At one time it seemed that Norwich, who had led the table for much of the season, might well steal the title from United. Robins began in style at Norwich, hitting the bulk of his goals in the early season, and many United supporters must have wondered why he had ever been sold. But the statistics probably told the tale. At United he had managed only 11 goals in 48 outings which was not the kind of goal rate United needed. In reserve and youth football he had been scoring at the rate of over 50 goals a season for a couple of years. He had joined United as an apprentice and was only 22 when he left. He was the first graduate of the FA National School to make an impact in league football. He scored the winning goal in the FA Cup semi-final to give United a place at Wembley in 1990.

ROBSON, BRYAN. If one man was to epitomise the United

Bryan Robson

side of the 1980s and early 90s, it was Bryan Robson, the Captain Marvel of Old Trafford. Commanding, daring, a defender, an attacker, a goalscorer and a fine team player, Robson had all the qualities that any manager longs for. He was born in the north-east yet somehow escaped the net of Newcastle and Sunderland and instead wound up at West Brom as a skinny, and rather small, 15 year old. He made his league debut for WBA in 1975 and then broke his leg three times the following year but rather than retire gracefully from the game Robson battled back to fitness each time. They were to be qualities he would show many times as injury dogged his career. Robson blossomed under the then West Brom manager Ron Atkinson and when Atkinson moved to Old Trafford one of the first decisions he made was to sign Robson for a British record fee of £1.5 million in October 1981. He was to prove not just Atkinson's best buy for United but one of the most astute purchases of the 1980s. Over the next 12 years Robson would go on to make well over 300 league appearances for United, leading the club to glory across Europe and at home. But the years and his combative spirit took their toll. He suffered shoulder dislocations, knee problems and even a broken ankle that led to him missing more than his fair share of games, both for United and England. He won his first England cap in 1980 while he was still with West Brom and 11 years later was still in the manager's plans as he neared a century of international honours. By then he was England's captain, starring in three World Cups. His greatest disappointment, however, was surely in the 1986 World Cup finals when he was helped from the field at a crucial moment with a dislocated shoulder that would eventually spell the end of England's World Cup dreams. Dogged by injury during the 1992–93 season, Robson came on against Blackburn Rovers in United's final home game of the season to crown his career with a league championship medal. He has also won FA Cup and European Cup-Winners' cup medals with the club.

ROBSON, JOHN, Manager, 1914–21. Officially Robson was the first-ever United manager in title as his predecessors, Ernest Mangnall and J. J. Bentley, went under the title of secretary. Robson took over the reins in 1914 after Bentley's uneasy period in office. Prior to coming to United, Robson had been in charge at Brighton and before that had been connected with Middlesbrough and Crystal Palace. Yet although Robson was to remain for seven years running the Old Trafford side, making him one of the longest ever serving United managers, his stay was hardly littered with treasures. True, United held on to the their first division spot but the glory years of the Edwardian era were now gone. War also intervened and much of Robson's period was spent supervising wartime games rather than competitive league football. As the fortunes of the club declined when league soccer resumed, Robson stepped aside and for a while remained as assistant to his successor John Chapman.

ROCCA, LOUIS. The man who dreamt up the name Manchester United. In 1902, following the club's bankruptcy, Newton Heath decided to change their name. They had moved from Newton Heath some years previously but there was still confusion and at least one team turned up at the wrong venue for a league match. A meeting was held to find another name. Various ideas were suggested, among them Manchester Central and Manchester Celtic but then Rocca put forward the name Manchester United and it was unanimously agreed. Rocca served with the club in many capacities but generally as a fixer. It was also Rocca who persuaded James Gibson in 1902 to put £2,000 into the club to save it from extinction. As if that was not enough it was Rocca who approached Matt Busby in 1945 to offer him the job as manager of United. For many years he was also chief scout at Old Trafford and was the man chiefly responsible for discovering so many of the Busby Babes.

ROWLEY, HENRY. Inside-forward of the inter-war years.

Rowley was unusual in that he enjoyed two separate spells with United. He originally joined the club in 1928 from non-league Shrewsbury Town, making his debut in his first season. He enjoyed a couple of good seasons with United, scoring 12 goals in 1929–30 as United lingered near the bottom of the table. But the following season when United were relegated the goals did not come so easily and after just one game in the second division he was sold to Manchester City. He found life at Maine Road just as difficult and two years later moved to second division Oldham. In 1934 he finally came back to United and enjoyed something of an Indian summer, scoring 19 goals in 1935–36 as United clinched the second division championship. But the following season, as United were again relegated, Rowley found the goals hard to come by and at the end of that season quit the game. He played 180 games in his two spells, scoring 55 goals.

ROWLEY, JACK. One of the most prolific goalscorers in United's history and one of the most remarkable of the immediate post-war period. It was undoubtedly Rowley's instinct for goal that gave United the edge over so many of their rivals and made them such a force in post-war soccer. Rowley was born in Wolverhampton and signed for Wolves but never matured beyond the Birmingham League. Third division Bournemouth, however, spotted the potential in him and signed him up in late 1936. Within a couple of months he had made his league debut and before the year was out had been transferred to United for £3,000. He was still only 19 years old and a week later was on the wing as United faced Sheffield Wednesday. After a bright start, however, he faded and spent the next six weeks in reserve football but then returned at centre-forward to knock in four goals as United thrashed Swansea 5–1. He was to hold on to the number nine shirt for the next 18 years. During his first season with the club United were promoted as the young man shot in nine goals. The following season he went one better but then war interrupted his career and he found himself guesting for a number of clubs including Wolves and Spurs, scoring eight in one game for Wolves and seven in another for Spurs. He kicked off the 1941–42 season playing with United and scored seven in his first match against New Brighton and ended the campaign having played 15 games and scored 34 goals. When peace returned he was back in the United line-up, scoring 28 goals in his first season. He had now matured into a strong, bustling centre-forward with a turn of pace and an eye for goal. Honours were showered on him. He played six times for England, winning his first cap against Switzerland in 1948 and his final cap in 1952 against Scotland. He also played for the England B side, the Football League and in a wartime international. And on top of that were his United honours. He won an FA Cup winners' medal in 1948 scoring twice as United beat Blackpool 4–2 and then struck a record-breaking 30 league goals as United clinched the championship in 1952. In all he hit 208 goals for United in 422 games, a goal every other match that has made him the third highest scorer in the club's history. After a glorious career with United Rowley joined Plymouth Argyle in 1955 as player-manager.

RUMBELOWS CUP. See **FOOTBALL LEAGUE CUP.**

RUNNERS UP. United have been first division runners up on ten occasions. When this is added to their eight championship titles it means that the club has finished in the top two in 18 years of its 100-year history. United have been runners up in:
1947, 1948, 1949, 1951, 1959, 1964, 1968, 1980, 1988 and 1992.

S

SADLER, DAVID. Before he joined United Sadler was already an England international – at amateur level. At the time he was playing with Maidstone United and was high on the wanted list of a number of clubs. But United won the race for his signature and Sadler, joining the club in November 1962, went on to enjoy 11 dazzling seasons at Old Trafford that brought him a bagful of honours. In a famous side Sadler was not always a star. He was quiet, unassuming and calm rather than spectacular. But it always had the desired result and his attitude brought a vital sense of calm to the United defence when it was most needed. United initially decided to convert him from a centre-half to a centre-forward and when he struck a hat-trick in the FA Youth Cup final in 1964 it seemed he was destined to become a big-scoring striker. But it never fully worked out that way. He began his United career by replacing David Herd upfront at the beginning of the 1963–64 season but the goals only arrived in dribs and drabs, five in 21 appearances and even less in subsequent years. Eventually he reverted to his favourite position, in the centre of defence, and began a far more fruitful association. It was where he always looked more comfortable and it also gave

THE OLD TRAFFORD ENCYCLOPEDIA

United the extra option of throwing a tall, pacey defender into attack when necessary. In 1967 he picked up a league championship medal and then a year later lined up at Wembley as United took on Benfica in the European Cup final. By then he was also adding to his England amateur international honours with three Under-23 caps and four full England caps. He won his first cap in 1967 against Northern Ireland with his final cap coming in 1970 against East Germany. Sadler ended his association with United in November 1973 when he joined Preston North End for £25,000. He played 326 games, scoring 27 goals.

SAGAR, CHARLES. One of the finest inside-forwards of his generation although he had known better days with Bury than with United. He joined the club from Bury in 1905, already an England international and the holder of a Cup winners' medal, even scoring the second goal in Bury's record-breaking shock 6–0 win over the famous Derby County. He enjoyed just two seasons with United, scoring at a staggering rate in his first season – 20 goals in just 23 appearances – as United clinched promotion from the second divison. Life back in the first division, however, was not so fruitful and he soon lost his place. At the end of that second season he left United and went into amateur football.

SCANDAL. The biggest scandal in United's history came on Good Friday 1915 when a game between United and Liverpool was fixed beforehand. United, facing relegation, were desperate for points, whereas Liverpool in mid-table had little to play for. But the real motive was not league points; instead it was to make money out of a betting coup. Bets were placed by some of the players, throughout the country on a score of 2–0 for United. And that was precisely how the game turned out. Not all the players were in on the deal but from the way the game was being played it was apparent not only to the players but also to the spectators that something was amiss. An FA inquiry later resulted in the suspension of eight players. The United culprits were Sandy Turnbull, Enoch West and Arthur Whalley although West was the only one to have actually played in the game. He always protested his innocence, however, even instigating a libel action that was to prove unsuccessful. The fixer was said to be Jackie Sheldon, a former United player who had been transferred to Liverpool. All were suspended but had their suspensions lifted after the war, except for West whose continual protests had clearly angered the footballing authorities.

SCANLON, ALBERT. The dashing Albert Scanlon never quite matured into the player he had always promised to become, perhaps affected by the horror of the Munich disaster in which he suffered severe injuries. Yet he recovered from the disaster and went on to play 127 games and score 35 goals for the club. Born in Manchester, he had joined United in much the same way as so many of the other Busby Babes. He starred in the 1953 and the 1954 Youth Cup winning sides and in November 1954 made his league debut against Arsenal. His appearances, however, continued to be limited over the next few seasons although he finally began to make the breakthrough into the first team shortly before the Munich disaster. He had enjoyed seven consecutive league appearances before United journeyed to Belgrade for the European Cup quarter-final match. Scanlon had appeared in the first leg against Red Star and also played in that second leg. The injuries which he suffered at Munich kept him out of action for the rest of that season but he returned for the beginning of the 1958–59 season and was ever present, scoring 16 goals. He enjoyed a couple more seasons on the United wing but late in 1960 signed for Newcastle in an £18,000 deal. Understandably, Munich seemed to have taken something out of him; the dash, the cheek, the confidence had all but disappeared. He later had spells with Lincoln and Mansfield.

SCHOFIELD, ALF. Liverpool-born Alf Schofield began his footballing days with Everton but never quite made the breakthrough with the Merseyside club. In 1900 after just 13 appearances he decided to try his luck elsewhere and joined United where he went on to enjoy a highly successful career, playing 179 games and scoring 35 goals. Schofield was an outside-right who became a vital part of United's second division winning side. But just as manager Ernest Mangnall was building his championship-winning side Schofield decided to retire. It was probably just as well as stepping into his boots was none other than Billy Meredith.

SCHMEICHEL, PETER. Following his impressive performance for Denmark as they won the European Championships in the summer of 1992, Peter Schmeichel was rated not only the best goalkeeper in the tournament but possibly the best in the world. And after winning the Premier League title in 1993 it's something United fans would not disagree with. He came to United in 1991 from the top Danish club Brondby for £600,000. In Denmark his popularity was phenomenal. In his final season with Brondby he had won two Player of the Year awards and been voted the third most popular person in Denmark in an opinion poll, ahead even of the Danish queen. In his first season at Old Trafford he kept 26 clean sheets in 53 games, helping United to win the League Cup and the European Super Cup. He began nervously with a few early mistakes that must have left a few people wondering if he really was as good as reports said. But his confidence soon grew and by the end of the season he was helping Denmark to their famous victory. In 1992–93 it was the presence of Schmeichel in goal that saved United on many an occasion with fingertip saves that eventually helped bring the championship back to Old Trafford after 26 years. He looks set to remain between the posts at United for many more years. At 6ft 4ins he is also one of the tallest goalkeepers in the Football League.

Peter Schmeichel

SCORES – HIGHEST. United's highest tally in any game is ten goals which they have scored on two occasions. Their best win was the 10–0 victory over Anderlecht of Belgium in the European Cup in September 1956. Their highest ever league victory came in October 1892 when they beat Wolverhampton Wanderers 10–1. United did, however, once achieve an even higher score, beating Walsall 14–0 in March 1895. That game, however, was to be declared null and void after Walsall complained about the state of the pitch. United won the replayed game 9–0. United's best post-war league score was the 8–1 defeat of Queens Park Rangers in March 1969. United's highest FA Cup win was the 8–0 victory over giantkillers Yeovil Town in February 1949. The Cup also brought United's highest ever away victory when they won 8–2 at Northampton Town in February 1970. During the war United beat New Brighton 13–1 with Jack Rowley scoring seven but given the teams and conditions during the war, such games and scores had little meaning.

SCOTLAND. There was a period during the 1970s, under Tommy Docherty's leadership, when United forged unusually close links with Scottish football. Docherty had come to United after a successful spell as manager of the Scottish national squad and consequently had a thorough knowledge of quality players at all levels in Scotland. Docherty bought a number of players he had groomed in Scotland to add to those already at Old Trafford. During this period United boasted Scottish internationals such as Martin Buchan, Jim Holton, George Graham, Alex Forsyth, Stewart Houston, Lou Macari and Willie Morgan with others such as Joe Jordan, Gordon Strachan and Gordon McQueen arriving shortly after Docherty's departure. Another United manager to have been in charge of the Scottish squad is Alex Ferguson although he has not employed the same policy as Docherty in bringing so many Scots to Old Trafford. Perhaps the finest ever Scot to play for United was Denis Law who won a total of 55 Scottish caps, scoring a record-breaking 30 goals for his country.

SEALEY, LES. United goalkeeper who was never able to secure his place. He made his name replacing Jim Leighton to star in United's FA Cup final victory over Crystal Palace in 1990. He served his apprenticeship with Coventry City and moved to Luton Town for £80,000 in June 1983 and had a loan spell with United before manager Alex Ferguson finally decided to sign him as a cover goalkeeper. He won a European Cup Winners' Cup medal in 1991. Unfortunately he never really got much beyond the role of understudy and the arrival of Danish keeper Peter Schmeichel signalled the end of his Old Trafford days. After a hectic 20 months at Old Trafford he signed for Aston Villa but returned to United in 1992.

SECOND DIVISION. United have had five spells in the second division. The first began in 1894 and lasted for twelve seasons before they won promotion in 1906. In 1922 they returned to the second division for three seasons and were relegated again in 1931, this time winning promotion in 1936. But that lasted just one season and they were back in the lower division. A season later, however, they returned to the first division and remained there until 1974 when Tommy Docherty's side were relegated. But again that was to last just one season as they clinched the second division championship in style. Since then they have remained in the higher division.

SEMI-FINALS. Up to the end of the 1992-93 season Manchester United had been involved in 18 FA Cup semi-finals.

SENDING OFFS. Former United man Liam O'Brien holds the record for one of the quickest sending offs in the first division when he was dismissed after just 85 seconds as United played Southampton in January 1987. United's Kevin Moran also had the dubious honour of being the first ever player to be sent off in an FA Cup final when he was dismissed for a somewhat clumsy tackle on Everton's Peter Reid in the 1985 Cup final at Wembley. United eventually won the match 1–0.

SETTERS, MAURICE. Tough, no-nonsense half-back of the early 1960s. Born in the West Country, Setters began his days with Exeter City but after only a handful of games was snapped up by West Bromwich Albion. He spent five years with the Midlands club before joining United in January 1960. By then he had won international honours at schoolboy, youth and Under-23 level. Setters was an instant success in the United team, a side sadly short of some fight in defence. Only days before he arrived they had conceded seven goals at Newcastle and since the start of the season had been leaking goals at the rate of two a game. Setters put that right. Few players went past him. He was as tough as they come, quick to the tackle and happy to venture where others feared. Generally, however, these were poor years for United, still suffering the tragic consequences of the Munich disaster. Setters's only honour at Old Trafford came in 1963 when United, reinforced by the arrival of Denis Law, beat Leicester City to win the FA Cup. By the time Busby had unearthed his world-beating team, Setters had gone. His final game was in October 1964 as United trounced Aston Villa 7–0. Weeks later he joined Stoke City for £30,000. He later had spells with Coventry and Charlton before trying his hand at management with Doncaster, Sheffield Wednesday and Rotherham. Despite his many qualities and his early grooming for full international honours, Setters never made the England team. In all he played 186 games for United, scoring 13 goals.

SEXTON, DAVE. United manager 1977–81. Dave Sexton looked the perfect answer to United's problems following the unseemly dismissal of Tommy Docherty. His record was impressive, having guided Chelsea to an FA Cup victory and a European Cup-Winners' Cup final and had then taken an unfashionable Queens Park Rangers to within sight of the league title. He was calm, thoughtful and articulate, with none of the cavalier of Docherty about him. Yet despite his pedigree and obvious coaching qualities Sexton's reign at Old Trafford failed to deliver the great prizes. He was appointed in July 1977 when everyone was predicting, including Arsenal, that he was heading for the manager's chair at Highbury. Sexton's first two seasons in charge at Old Trafford brought little except a Cup final appearance against Arsenal but in his third season United at least gave Liverpool a run for their money to finish as runners up. But that was never going to satisfy the United directors, nor the Stretford Enders. Docherty, for all his trouble, had at least brought a whiff of glamour and adventure to Old Trafford. Under Sexton life seemed drab and dreary by comparison. He made a few intelligent buys, especially Ray Wilkins, Joe Jordan and Gordon McQueen but had also spent heavily on Garry Birtles who proved a disastrous and costly failure. On balance £3.5 million had been spent and only £1.5 million recouped. At the end of the day Sexton seemed all too similar to Frank O'Farrell and in April 1981 he was sacked even though United had just ended the season winning eight consecutive games.

SHARPE, LEE. Signed from Torquay where, after just a handful of games, he had every club in the first division

Lee Sharpe

scrambling for his signature. United won the race and the youngster has gone on to show that he has the potential to mature into an outstanding player. He came into the United side near the start of the 1988–89 campaign but injuries soon interrupted his career. Two hernia operations initially halted his progress and then viral meningitis further interrupted his game. But he came back bravely and during the 1992–93 season helped swing the championship in United's direction. In 1991 he was named Young Player of the Year and has already come into international reckoning with a substitute appearance against the Republic of Ireland. He played against Barcelona in the European Cup-Winners' Cup final and came on as a substitute at Wembley as United beat Nottingham Forest to win the League Cup.

SILCOCK, JOHN. Full-back of the inter-war years. Born in Wigan, Silcock joined United in 1916 as an amateur and went on to play 449 games for the club before retiring 18 years later in 1934. He made his debut as soon as league football kicked off again after the First World War, having already played more than a century of wartime games. Silcock was an impressive full-back with a sure foot and a strong head. For many years he and Charlie Moore were the obvious choice in the United defence. Yet, for all their qualities, Silcock and Moore allowed more than their fair share of strikers to get past them. They were not outstanding years for United and it was a mark of Silcock's quality that he should be capped three times by England, winning his first cap in 1921, and also made three appearances for the Football League. He also starred in the North of England team that thrashed a full England side 6–1 in a trial match in 1921.

SIVEBAEK, JOHNNY. The second Danish player to join United after Jesper Olsen. Sivebaek made his United debut in February 1986 but did not enjoy much of the success of his predecessor. A footballing full-back, Sivebaek liked to play himself out of trouble though on occasions he was also caught in possession. He played just 32 games for United before joining the French club St Etienne in 1987. Sivebaek won 11 caps for Denmark while he was with United.

SMALLEST PLAYER. Although such statistics are always unreliable and were generally not even available for those playing before 1900, the distinction of being United's smallest player probably rests with Ernie Taylor who joined the club immediately after the Munich disaster. Taylor was just 5ft 4ins.

SOUTH AFRICA. Over the years United have boasted a number of South African-born players on their books. One of the most famous was Alex Bell, an outstanding wing-half of the Edwardian era who helped United to two league championships and the FA Cup. Bell had been born in South Africa of Scottish parents and went on to play more than 300 games for the club. Another man with South African connections was Gary Bailey. Although he was actually born in Ipswich, Bailey spent much of his youth in South Africa and was spotted while playing for Witts University.

SPENCE, JOE. For many years Joe Spence held the record for the number of appearances for United. In his 14 seasons at Old Trafford between 1919 and 1933 he made just over 500 appearances, scoring 168 goals. It was a record that stood for 40 years until beaten by Bill Foulkes. Born in Northumberland, Spence came to United straight from amateur football and made his debut as soon as soccer resumed at the end of the First World War. Spence was able to play in almost any forward position though he was most at home either on the right wing or at centre-forward. He was a useful rather than a spectacular goalscorer and was top marksman in his first season with United and top scorer in seven subsequent seasons. In June 1933 he joined Bradford City and later had a spell with Chesterfield before retiring in 1938. He played a total of 510 games for United,

481 of these in the league.

SPONSORS. United are almost unique in the Football League in having had the same sponsors since sponsorship was allowed. United were also one of the first clubs in the Football League to announce a sponsorship deal when Sharp became their official sponsors in 1979.

STACEY, GEORGE. Over the years Barnsley have had a tradition of unearthing some of the toughest of defenders and in George Stacey they produced someone without equal for his time. Stacey had originally joined Sheffield Wednesday but failing to establish himself had moved to Barnsley. There in the school of hard Yorkshire football he began to emerge as one of the hardest defenders. Stacey had originally been a coalminer and in 1907 he was snapped up by United as they began their assault on the league title. Over the years Stacey was to prove an enormous asset, sweeping up anything which might have slipped past centre-half Charlie Roberts. Stacey had begun life as a right-back but was converted to a left-back while at United. In the eight seasons he was with United, until the outbreak of the First World War, Stacey played 241 games for the club, won two league championship medals and an FA Cup winners' medal. While Roberts, Meredith and others were the stars of this great United side, Stacey was one of the unsung heroes.

STAFFORD, HARRY. Without Harry Stafford Manchester United would almost certainly not be in existence today. For it was Stafford, or rather his dog, who was responsible for introducing John Davies to the club. It was Stafford who returned Davies's lost dog to him. And it was Davies's money which was to prove United's lifeline when the club was bankrupted in 1902. Stafford had joined the club when it was still known as Newton Heath, back in 1895. He was a full-back from Crewe and served the club for eight seasons, playing exactly 200 games for the club, many of them as skipper. When the club was bankrupted Stafford campaigned as much as anyone to help save them from extinction, often sacrificing his training just to keep the club afloat. His loyalty was eventually rewarded when he was made a director but in 1911, suffering from ill health, he decided to emigrate. United gave him £50 towards his travel expenses – little recompense considering they really owed their existence to him.

STAPLETON, FRANK. As a teenager Frank Stapleton was on United's books but someone, in their wisdom, decided he had no future at Old Trafford and the youngster was allowed to drift away. He eventually wound up at Highbury and a number of years later cost United £1 million when they signed him from Arsenal. By then Stapleton had won international honours and a number of medals leading the Arsenal attack. A strong, combative centre-forward, Stapleton was always prepared to battle away upfront, brave enough to go where others feared. Born in Dublin, he signed for United in August 1981 having played some 200 games for the Gunners and went on to play many more for United. He was not always the most prolific of goalscorers but his very presence in the opposing penalty area was always sufficient to cause panic and confusion among defenders. He eventually left United in 1988 and later had spells with Derby County, Le Havre and Blackburn Rovers. He was capped 70 times by the Republic of Ireland, winning his first cap in 1977 and his final cap in 1990. At United he became the first player to ever score for different clubs in a Wembley Cup final when he scored against Brighton in the 1983 Cup final.

STEPNEY, ALEX. Of all the goalkeepers in United's long history, Alex Stepney will always rank among the most popular and respected. He came to Old Trafford after a disastrous spell at Chelsea. Signed by Chelsea manager Tommy Docherty for £50,000 from Millwall, Stepney made only one appearance and was then sold just months later to

United for £55,000. At least Chelsea made a profit but given the magnificent service that Stepney gave to United, Chelsea might later have regretted not giving him a little more encouragement. He joined United in late 1966 and immediately stepped into the first team and from then on was the automatic choice. In his first season United lifted the championship and then a season later the European Cup with Stepney making at least one spectacular save from Eusebio in the dying moments of normal time in the final against Benfica. He went on to enjoy 535 games for United and even scored a couple of goals from the penalty spot in United's relegation season 1973–74. At one point he was actually leading goalscorer. He also won an FA Cup winners' medal in 1977 as United beat Liverpool in the final to deny them the double. He was capped just once by England in 1968 against Sweden and although he was also chosen for the 1970 World Cup squad he never actually played. After 12 seasons' loyal service he left United and joined the trek to the United States.

STEWARD, ALF. Goalkeeper signed shortly after the First World War but who made only a handful of appearances until 1923 when he eventually succeeded John Mew as United's first choice in goal. Steward was a local lad playing with Stalybridge Celtic when he was signed though he probably never imagined that he would have to wait so long for his opportunity. But once he had settled into the position he was to give good service to the club as regular custodian until 1932. A fine goalkeeper, Steward was unfortunate to be at Old Trafford as the last line of defence in such an indifferent team. He left the club in 1932 and later became manager at Torquay. He played 326 games for United.

STILES, NOBBY. The United midfielder will always be remembered for his chirpy, toothless smile following England's famous World Cup victory in 1966 but United supporters will also remember him for his terrier-like performances week after week. Stiles was the supreme competitor, always giving 100 per cent, always committed to the United cause. He never lost heart, he never gave up, he knew only how to battle and United's successes of the 1960s owed as much to his persistence and endeavour as it did to the lavish skills of others. Although he was on the short side, he more than made up for his lack of height with unbounding enthusiasm. Born in Manchester, he joined United as a schoolboy in 1957, turning professional two years later. He was still only 18 when he made his debut in 1960 and went on to play 363 games in his 14 years at Old Trafford. What's more he picked up almost every honour in the game – a World Cup winners' medal, a European Cup winners' medal and two league championship medals, plus 28 full England caps and a clutch more at schoolboy, youth and Under-23 level. Only the FA Cup and the League Cup evaded him. He finally quit United in 1971 when he was transferred to Middlesbrough for £20,000. Two years later he joined his former United colleague Bobby Charlton at Preston but despite their enormous pedigree the pair could not turn the fortunes of this once great club. Stiles later had a spell as manager at Preston and in the USA as well as at West Bromwich Albion. He is now back at United, coaching.

STRACHAN, GORDON. The Scottish midfielder was in much the same mould as Nobby Stiles, short, tenacious and above all enthusiastic. Strachan arrived at Old Trafford in the wake of Ray Wilkin's sale to Milan. He had been expected to sign for Cologne but at the last moment United manager, Ron Atkinson put in a smart £600,000 bid for the flame-haired Scottish international. The experienced Strachan proved a good buy although given his later glory with Leeds United some may wonder if United ever really got the best out of him. Strachan had begun his career with Dundee but had moved to Aberdeen in November 1977 where he helped the Scottish club under Alex Ferguson to a clutch of honours. He was soon in the hunt for further

Gordon Strachan

honours at Old Trafford, adding an FA Cup winners' medal to his collection in 1985. Strachan brought much the same endeavour and passion to the United midfield as Stiles had in earlier years and went on to play more than 150 games, scoring 33 goals. The eventual arrival of his former manager Alex Ferguson, however, brought a swift end to his United days. The two men were known not to see eye to eye and in March 1989 Strachan waved farewell to Old Trafford, joining Leeds United. Two seasons later Leeds, inspired by the ageing Strachan, pipped United to the league title. He was capped more than 50 times by Scotland.

STRETFORD END. For so many years the home of the most raucous and vociferous of United supporters. The mass terracing at one end of the ground was famous throughout the world of soccer for its singing and fanatical support. It could hold as many as 15,000 fans but in 1992 it was pulled down and a major reconstruction programme began to seat the entire area.

SUBSTITUTES. The first ever United substitute was John Fitzpatrick who came on for Denis Law on 16 October 1965 when United played at Tottenham.

SUPER CUP. United have played in the European Super Cup on just one occasion, beating the European Cup holders Red Star Belgrade 1–0 in a one-off match at Old Trafford.

SUTCLIFFE, JOHN. Edwardian goalkeeper who was a soccer and rugby international. By the time Sutcliffe joined United he was already past his best days, having kept goal for Bolton in the 1894 Cup final and won his five England caps. He came to United in 1903 and had just one season between the sticks as United narrowly missed out on promotion. At the end of that season he joined Plymouth Argyle and later coached at Southend and on the continent.

T

TALLEST. It is impossible to say for definite who has been the tallest ever player on United's books but two men certainly competing for that distinction must be Gary Pallister and Peter Schmeichel who are both 6ft 4ins.

TAYLOR, ERNIE. Following the Munich disaster United were left desperately short of players. Not only had eight United players died in the air crash but others were seriously injured and unlikely to play for some time, if at all. United needed to recruit players immediately and one of the first to be signed was Ernie Taylor, the 5ft 4ins Blackpool inside-forward. Taylor was vastly experienced with more than 300 league games to his name and a couple of FA Cup winners' medals with Newcastle and Blackpool. Although he was 33 years old he was just what United needed and Blackpool sold him to United for just £8,000. Taylor made his debut for United days later against Sheffield Wednesday in the highly emotional FA Cup game and he went on to play in all the subsequent Cup games that season including the Wembley final. He also played 11 league matches and appeared in both legs of United's European Cup semi-final against AC Milan. Taylor remained with United until the end of 1958 when Sunderland paid £6,000 for him. He later returned briefly to the Manchester area, joining Altrincham. In all he had played just 30 games for United, scoring four goals, but his contribution, which came at such a desperate time for United, should never be underestimated.

TAYLOR, TOMMY. Jack Rowley and Bobby Charlton may have scored many more goals than Tommy Taylor but ask older United fans who was the club's greatest goalscorer and the answer will inevitably be Tommy Taylor. In just 189 games for the club Taylor scored a staggering 128 goals. He was without much doubt the finest goalscorer in British football during the 1950s and as United's exploits in Europe showed, there were few who were his equal on the Continent. Taylor was born in Barnsley and signed professional forms with his local club in 1949. He was soon knocking in the goals, 26 in 44 games at Barnsley, though usually as an inside-forward. In March 1953 Busby paid Barnsley £29,999 for the young man and quickly converted him into an out-and-out scoring centre-forward. Taylor was devastating. He had everything: quicksilver pace, a ferocious shot, a powerful heading ability, and a goalscorer's instinct for position. The goals came easily and rapidly, helped admittedly by the wing work of David Pegg and Johnny Berry plus the scheming of Dennis Viollet who was almost as prolific. In his first season he scored seven goals in 11 outings. His best season was 1956–57 as United clinched the championship and Taylor netted a season's total of 34. By then he was also an established England international. He won his first cap in 1953 against Argentina and went on to collect 18 more before his untimely death at Munich. Taylor played twice in the 1954 World Cup finals in Switzerland though the England selectors still preferred the more experienced Nat Lofthouse. Yet it was Taylor's goals which paved the way for England's qualification in the next World Cup finals. It was one of the great tragedies of English football that England had to venture into those finals without three of their greatest stars – the United trio of Byrne, Edwards and Taylor. With them England would almost certainly have progressed beyond the quarter-finals. In just 19 games for England Taylor scored 16 goals.

TEST MATCHES. During the latter years of the nineteenth century promotion and relegation battles were settled by a series of play-offs, known as Test Matches. At the end of their first ever season in the Football League United, or Newton Heath as they then were, finished in bottom position and went into a play-off match with Small Heath (later to be called Birmingham City) who had topped the second division. United were expected to lose but surprisingly won 5–2 after drawing their first encounter 1–1. The following season found United in much the same position, bottom of the first division, and forced into the play-offs. But this time they were unlucky, losing 2–0 to Liverpool who had finished top of the second division. United were duly relegated. A season later United once more found themselves in the play-offs, this time after topping the second division. They faced Stoke but unfortunately lost 0–3 and had to face another season in the lower division. Their next encounter with the play-offs came two seasons later in 1897. United had finished up in second spot and went into a mini league with the bottom two of the first division and the top club from the second division. But United did not play well and finished up in third place and so remained in the second division.

THOMAS, HENRY. Welsh-born outside-left who played with United during the inter-war years. Henry joined the club from the Welsh side Porth in April 1922 and went on to play 135 games, scoring 13 goals, and remained with United until 1931. He was capped just once by Wales in 1927.

THOMAS, MICKEY. Joined United from Wrexham in November 1978 for £300,000 but remained only three years at Old Trafford which at least was longer than he had with most clubs. He was a useful little winger who liked to cut inside and strike for goal. He had pace, cunning and was never afraid to take on defenders. But Thomas could never really settle anywhere and after United had spells with Everton, Chelsea, Stoke, West Brom and Derby before returning to Wrexham. The only consistency in Thomas's footballing career was his regular selection for Wales. He was capped more than 50 times, winning his first honour in 1977. In all he played 110 games for United, scoring 15 goals before he was sold to Everton in 1981 in part exchange for John Gidman.

TOURS. United were early pioneers of international tours. The first ever close-season tour which they made was in 1908 following their league championship triumph. The club went on a tour of the Austro-Hungarian Empire, playing in Vienna, Prague and then Budapest. In Hungary they played a couple of matches against Ferencvaros, both of which proved to be particularly stormy. United won the first encounter 6–2 but in the second game played a few days later there was a near riot when United swept into a two-goal lead. Before the final whistle had been blown three United players had been sent off and interpreters had to intervene as the referee threatened to abandon the match. Yet despite all the problems United still won 7–0. The real trouble began after the final whistle when the crowd began hurling stones at the players. Fearing a riot, the Hungarian police drew their swords and rushed the crowd. Later, as the team made its way back to the city, they were again attacked by a stone-throwing crowd, estimated to be in the region of several thousand. Two United players were struck on the head and only a further sword-drawn attack and scores of arrests by the police saved United from the mob. Thankfully there have been no further repeats of such behaviour on United's foreign tours which have since taken in most corners of the globe.

TRANSFERS, RECORD. United have broken the British transfer record on a number of occasions, the most spectacular being the £115,000 paid to the Italian club Torino for the Scottish international Denis Law in July 1962. It was the first time any British club had ever paid a six-figure fee for a footballer. United also spent heavily in August 1989, paying Middlesbrough a British record fee of £2.3 million for the giant defender Gary Pallister. In July 1993 they again broke the transfer record when they paid £3.75 million for the Nottingham Forest midfielder Roy Keane.

TURNBULL, SANDY. One of the great inside-forwards of the Edwardian era who was tragically killed during the First World War. Turnbull joined United from Manchester City in 1906 along with Meredith and others after the City players had been suspended for taking illegal payments. Turnbull was an exceptional goalscorer. He had joined City from Hurlford in 1902 and scored 60 goals in 119 games with them. But it was with United that he really excelled, scoring a century of goals in 245 games. He played right through until the outbreak of war, winning league championship, FA Cup and second division medals with the club. He even scored United's winning goal in the 1909 Cup final against Bristol City and as United picked up their first league title Turnbull was top marksman with 25 league goals. In 1915 Turnbull was one of several United players to be suspended by the Football League after his involvement in the betting scandal that rocked the club. Sadly, he was to be killed in action in France in May 1917.

TURNER, CHRIS. United goalkeeper who made his debut in December 1985, taking over from Gary Bailey. Turner had been bought from Sunderland for what was then a club record fee for a goalkeeper of £250,000. But with Gary Bailey in magnificent form Turner had to wait until Bailey was injured before claiming his place. He then wore the keeper's jersey until February 1987 when young Gary Walsh was given his chance. He left the club in 1988 after 79 games.

U

UEFA CUP. Originally known as the Fairs Cup but changed its name in 1971 to become the UEFA Cup. United first participated in the UEFA Cup in 1976 when they met and defeated the great Dutch club Ajax. Unfortunately they were knocked out in the next round by Juventus. They again participated in the 1980–81 season but went out in the first round to Widzew Lodz. Their third appearance came during the1982–83 season when they were knocked out by Valencia in the first round. United were luckier during the 1984–85 season when they battled their way through to the quarter-finals before going out to Videoton on penalties but the competition remains the only European tournament that United have never won.

UNDEFEATED – AT HOME. United have had a number of seasons when they have been undefeated at home. They were 1894–95, 1896–97, 1955–56, 1966–67 and 1982–83.

UNDEFEATED – FROM START OF SEASON. From the start of the 1985–86 season United notched up ten consecutive victories before they finally dropped a point. It was not until their sixteenth game that they lost a match.

This was the best start ever in the club's history.

UNIVERSITY. A number of United players have had university educations, perhaps the most notable being Steve Coppell who attended Manchester University and Alan Gowling who attended the same university while he was on United's books.

V

VICTORIES IN A SEASON – HIGHEST. United's highest number of league victories in a season is 28. This has been achieved twice, in 1905–06 when they won the second division title, and in 1956–57 when they finished as league champions.

VICTORIES IN A SEASON – LOWEST. United's poorest performances were in 1892–93 and 1893–94. In each of those seasons they won just six games. Indeed they went 18 months without an away victory. But with only 30 games a season played, comparisons are a little unfair. United's worst campaign under the 42-fixtures-a-season regime was undoubtedly 1930–31 when they finished bottom of the first division having won just seven games. They managed only one win away from home that season.

VICTORY INTERNATIONALS. United have had a number of players who represented their country in the victory internationals. Charlie Mitten and Joe Walton played in the Bolton Disaster Fund game against Scotland in 1946 while Joe Delaney played twice for Scotland in 1946. Irish internationals included Johnny Carey and Tom Breen. Just after the First World War Clarrie Hilditch played for England in a victory international while Billy Meredith played twice for Wales. O'Connell also played for Ireland in 1919.

VIDEOS. United have produced a number of videos in conjunction with the BBC, the most notable being an official history of the club.

VIOLLET, DENNIS. When all the great United names are remembered, the one most often forgotten is that of Dennis Viollet. Yet Viollet's contribution to the United cause is equal to almost anyone's, with the possible exceptions of Meredith and Charlton. Born in Manchester in 1933, Viollet joined the club as a 16-year-old and went on to give them 13 years of unstinting, loyal service. In that time he played almost 300 games, scoring an impressive 178 goals. He made his debut in April 1953 when he was still only 19 and finally left the club in January 1962, signing for Stoke in a £25,000 deal. In between he had picked up two league championship medals with the great Busby Babes side and an FA Cup runners up medal as well. Viollet survived the Munich disaster although he was badly injured but was back at Old Trafford playing football before the season was out, even appearing in the Wembley final against Bolton Wanderers that year. Viollet was a classic 1950s inside-forward: pacey, powerful, an accurate passer of the ball and with an eye for goal. He scored 20 or more goals in six consecutive seasons and his 32 league goals during the 1959–60 season still remains a club record. During the 1956–57 season he also netted nine goals in Europe to set another club record, four of them coming in the 10–0 thrashing of Anderlecht. Yet for all his goals and undoubted ability, Viollet was capped only twice by his country, making his England debut in 1960 against Hungary and then in 1961 lining up against Luxembourg. After leaving United, Viollet joined Stoke City where he went on to make 182 appearances and score 59 goals. He finally quit Stoke in

1966 and then travelled around, playing in Ireland and America before trying his hand at coaching and management.

VOSE, GEORGE. St Helens-born Vose came to Old Trafford during the lean years of the 1930s, though had some of his colleagues possessed just a snip of his ability, United would surely not have struggled so much. Vose made his debut at the beginning of the 1933–34 season, a year after joining United and went on to make 211 appearances for the club. A strong, straightforward centre-half, Vose played the game simply. Fancy footwork and tricks were for inside-forwards; defenders got rid of the ball quickly, though Vose always performed his task with composure and authority. Up until the war he was a regular choice but the outbreak of war effectively ended his footballing career. By the time hostilities had ceased he was gone, joining Cheshire League club Runcorn. Vose ended his United days with only a second division championship medal to show for all his endeavours. There had been little to cheer about during his years at the club with promotion invariably followed by relegation. Vose was a player who deserved better and who, alongside equally talented players, might have gone on to win England honours.

WALL, GEORGE. Another product of the Barnsley school of football. Wall was born in the north-east but went to play for Barnsley in 1902. Four years later he was spotted by Louis Rocca and promptly signed for United. It was to be the beginning of a productive ten years that would stretch to the First World War. During that time Wall made 316 appearances for the club, scoring almost a century of goals. He also picked up a couple of championship medals and an FA Cup winners' medal as well as seven England caps. His first international honour came in 1907 and his final cap in 1913. Wall was a tough winger who could ride tackles, had a ferocious shot and was a useful goalscorer. He was a vital part of United's all-out attacking forward line, playing alongside the legendary Billy Meredith and Sandy Turnbull. Had war not broken out, Wall would no doubt have played many more games for United. As it was, he signed for Oldham at the end of the war and played with them for a couple of seasons before joining Hamilton Academicals. He later had a brief spell with Rochdale before retiring in 1923.

WALLACE, DANNY. Winger signed from Southampton for £1.2 million in September 1989. The 25-year-old Wallace was a midfielder, brought in to bring some width to the side. He had played 255 league games with the Saints, scoring 64 goals, but he was never quite as potent or dangerous for United. He began as a regular in the United line-up but the emergence of Ryan Giggs has since limited his appearances. He has played just over 50 games for the club and has been capped once by England, in 1986 against Egypt when he scored in England's 4–0 win. He made 14 appearances for England Under-21s. His brothers Ray and Rodney both played with him at Southampton.

WALSH, GARY. United goalkeeper who made his debut in 1986. He came into football through the government's YTS project and signed professional forms in December 1986. Walsh has so far made just over 40 appearances for the club. He took over from Chris Turner mid-way through the 1986–87 season and held his place for almost 12 months until he was concussed in a game against Sheffield Wednesday and Chris Turner again became the number-one choice. The arrival of Jim Leighton and then Peter Schmeichel have, however, limited his appearances since then. He played just two games in United's championship season but none in the league.

WAR. United have lost a number of players fighting for their country. During the First World War Sandy Turnbull, one of their greatest ever centre-forwards, was killed in action in France in May 1917. Another famous United player, Arthur Whalley, was wounded although he recovered and returned to play for United for a season after the war. The Second World War also brought its casualties. Ben Carpenter, who had joined the club just before the outbreak of war, lost his life, while Johnny Hanlon and Allenby Chilton were both wounded.

WAR DAMAGE. On the night of Tuesday 11 March 1941 a major bombing raid on Trafford Park resulted in at least one bomb being dropped on the Old Trafford ground and causing extensive damage. It meant the end of football at Old Trafford for some time and United were forced to borrow City's ground at Maine Road to continue their wartime fixtures. After the war they continued to play at Maine Road which proved a lucky ground for them and they did not return to Old Trafford until 1949 when repairs had finally been completed.

WARTIME FOOTBALL. Like most clubs United continued to play football during both wars even though the normal Football League programme had been suspended. During the First World War they played in the Lancashire section of the league but were not very successful. In the Second World War they again played in a regional league, this time the Football League North. There was also a guesting system which allowed players from other clubs to play for a side close to where they were barracked. They recorded a number of high scores including a 13–1 win over New Brighton, 10–3 against Wrexham and 8–1 against Chester, all in the same season.

WARTIME INTERNATIONALS. United boast only one wartime international. He was Jack Rowley who played for England against Wales in 1944. Rowley also played in a wartime inter-league match for the Football League against the Scottish League in 1944.

WARNER, JOHN. Wing-half John Warner's career spanned the immediate periods before and after the Second World War. Like so many players his best days were during the war and had war not brought an end to league football he might well have become one of the great names at the club. As it was, he played only 118 games for United, despite being on their books for 12 years. He joined United from Swansea in June 1938 and immediately stepped into the first team. After the war he was still able to hold down a first-team place and even in 1949–50 made 25 appearances. But that was to be his final season. He then moved to Oldham and later to Rochdale. He did not feature in United's 1948 Cup winning side but did at least add another Welsh international cap to the one he had already won at Swansea.

WATNEY CUP. United competed for the Watney Cup in both 1970 and 1971. In the first year they reached the final only to be beaten 1–4 by Derby County. The following year they were eliminated in the first round, beaten 1–2 by Halifax Town.

WEBSTER, COLIN. Busby Babe whose appearances were limited until after the Munich air disaster. Welsh-born Webster began his footballing days with Cardiff City but failed to make the breakthrough and was signed by United in May 1952. He made his United debut during the 1953–54 season but with so much talent around Old Trafford his appearances were to be occasional rather than regular. He did, however, make 15 league appearances in the United side that clinched the championship in 1956 and thereby qualified for a championship medal. A utility player, his real chance came after the Munich disaster and he went on to play 31 games that season, including the FA Cup final. He signed for Swansea in October 1958, having played 79 games for United with an impressive 31 goals. He won four Welsh caps, most of them during the 1958 World Cup finals.

WEBB, NEIL. Stylish midfielder signed from Nottingham Forest for £1.5 million in June 1989. A regular England international, Webb was a major signing whose contract at Forest had run out. He had little hesitation in teaming up with his England colleague Bryan Robson and there were high hopes that with Webb and Robson running the United engine-room the title would soon be on its way to Old Trafford. But of course it never quite worked out that way. Webb's career had begun with Reading before he signed for Portsmouth in 1982. He joined Brian Clough's Nottingham Forest three years later and after 18 England caps

Neil Webb

eventually arrived in Manchester. Unfortunately his United career was to be dogged by injury. After just a few games at the beginning of the 1989–90 season he damaged an achilles tendon while playing for England and many thought it might spell the end of his career but he fought back to regain his place by the end of the season and was in the United side that won the FA Cup. But there was no doubt that the injury had taken its toll. He seemed to have lost some of his speed and although he continued to line up for United he was never quite the same player. He won another eight caps while at United but then in 1992 he found his place under threat and after a disagreement with manager Alex Ferguson he returned to Nottingham Forest.

WEMBLEY. Wembley has become almost a second home to United. Up to the end of the 1992–93 season they had played there on 21 occasions in major games, having made 12 appearances in the FA Cup final (including replays), three in the League Cup final, five in the Charity Shield and one in a European Cup final.

WEST, ENOCH. Impressive goalscorer in the years immediately prior to the First World War. West joined the club in the summer of 1910 and helped United to win their second league championship in his first season, scoring 19 league goals. Born in Nottingham, he had first played with Nottingham Forest where his goalscoring instincts made him one of the league's top marksmen. His career with United, however, was to end under a black cloud as he was given a life suspension for his part in the fixing of a game against Liverpool on Good Friday 1915. In all he had played 181 games for United, scoring 80 goals.

WHALLEY, ARTHUR. Centre-half of the Edwardian era. Unfortunately United already had one of the finest centre-halves of the time in Charlie Roberts and Whalley's appearances were restricted for many years. Eventually Roberts left to join Oldham and Whalley was given his

THE OLD TRAFFORD ENCYCLOPEDIA

opportunity. He had joined the club from Blackpool in 1909. He played just enough games in the 1910–11 season to warrant a league championship medal. After the war he returned to Old Trafford and played 25 games in that first season following hostilities. During the summer of 1920, after just over 100 games for United, he left to join Southend United and then moved to Charlton.

WHALLEY, BERT. United player and coach who died in the Munich air disaster. Whalley played for United before, during and after the Second World War. He made just 33 league appearances for the club although he played almost 200 times during the war. A half-back or defender, Whalley took up a coaching appointment with United after the war and was partly responsible for helping to develop so many of United's fine youngsters. He was not scheduled to go on the United trip to Belgrade but with assistant manager Jimmy Murphy tied up with international duties, Whalley volunteered to go along. Sadly he was killed in the disaster.

WHELAN, BILL. Busby Babe killed in the Munich air disaster. Born in Dublin, Whelan joined United from Home Farm in 1953 and soon established himself as an accomplished inside-forward. He was also a prolific goal-scorer, netting 52 goals in just 96 games for United. With Taylor and Viollet playing alongside him, United had one of the most dangerous forward lines British soccer has ever seen with any one of them capable of hitting 20 goals and more a season. During United's championship season of 1956–57, Whelan struck 26 league goals in 39 games with Taylor hitting 22. Whelan collected championship medals in both 1956 and 1957 and appeared in the 1957 FA Cup final. He had a delightful touch, bringing elegance and skill to the United attack. And yet despite his many qualities, his place in the side was always under threat with a young Bobby Charlton knocking on the door. Indeed, it was Charlton who won their private battle to play against Red

Star in the European Cup but Whelan still made the trip and sadly died in the crash at Munich. He was capped four times by the Republic of Ireland.

WHITEFOOT, JEFF. Has the honour of being the youngest ever league player for United when at 16 years and 105 days old he made his league debut against Portsmouth in April 1950. Whitefoot had joined the club the previous year and played with them for seven seasons, making 95 appearances. His best year was 1953–54 when he played 39 times. He made just enough appearances in the 1955–56 season to give him a championship medal but after that he lost his place at right-half to Eddie Colman and a year later decided on a move to Grimsby. The following season he moved to Nottingham Forest where he enjoyed ten years of football, winning an FA Cup winners' medal.

WHITESIDE, NORMAN. Another record-breaking youngster who became the youngest ever scorer in both an FA Cup final and a League Cup final. Whiteside followed in the tradition of so many United youngsters, making his debut when he was still only a 16 year old. He came on as a substitute at Brighton in April 1982. Even at that age he was tall, strong and powerful, not unlike Duncan Edwards. It was his only appearance that season but the following year he quickly established himself as a regular and remained a favourite with United until the arrival of Alex Ferguson. At 17 he also became the youngest ever player in the final stages of the World Cup when he played for Northern Ireland in Spain in 1982. Whiteside's talent was in his strength and his ability to carry the ball into the penalty area. He was a difficult man to dispossess and was as tough a tackler as anyone in the Football League. It may not have won him too many friends outside Old Trafford but he was effective. He also had an eye for goal and it was his shot in the 1985 Cup final against Everton which won the game for United. After more than 200 league games for United with 47 goals he was surprisingly sold to Everton. His

Norman Whiteside

appearances at Goodison, however, were to be limited by injury and in 1992 he decided to call it a day and retired, still only in his mid-twenties. Whiteside was first capped by Northern Ireland in 1982 after just a handful of games for United. In all he went on to win 38 caps, all but two of them while he was a United player.

WILKINS, RAY. When United manager Dave Sexton signed Ray Wilkins for a club-record fee of £825,000 in August 1979, there were high hopes that Wilkins would be the man to bring elegance and winning ways to Old Trafford. It was Sexton who had originally signed the young 15-year-old Wilkins for Chelsea and it was hardly surprising that Sexton should turn once again to his protégé for inspiration.

THE OLD TRAFFORD ENCYCLOPEDIA

Wilkins came with a pedigree as long as his arm. He already had 24 England caps and had skippered Chelsea to promotion. He was a fine captain and it was not long before he was skipper of United and England. Wilkins thrived on responsibility, always leading from the front. He was articulate, charming and above all a supreme professional and although he took a little time to settle at Old Trafford, he was soon the fulcrum of the United midfield. He won an FA Cup winners' medal against Brighton in 1983 but then a year later left United to join AC Milan for £1.5 million. By then Sexton had gone and Wilkins had lost the captaincy to Bryan Robson and was beginning to see his future elsewhere. He later joined Paris St Germain and then Glasgow Rangers but returned to England to join Queens Park Rangers. He won 38 caps with United to give him a grand total of 84 caps.

WILSON, JOHN. Began his football at the top, worked his way down and then with United suddenly reappeared at the top. That just about sums up John Wilson's career. He started with Newcastle United, playing in the first division just after the First World War but then played with Durham and Stockport in the third division before United tempted him back into first division soccer. He then went on to enjoy six seasons at Old Trafford, playing 140 games, the vast majority in the first division. In his penultimate season United were relegated and after just nine games the following season in division two he was sold to Bristol City.

WINS – SUCCESSIVE. United, along with Bristol City and Preston North End hold the record for the number of successive wins in league football. In January 1905 they achieved their fourteenth successive league win and became the first club to break the record of 13 league wins. Their record was equalled later that year by Bristol City and then by Preston in 1951. All three clubs achieved their 14 victories in the second division.

WINTERBOTTOM, WALTER. Better known as the England manager than for his United career. Lancashire-born Winterbottom came to Old Trafford in the mid-1930s. At the time he was working as a school teacher and playing local football but United gave him a chance in the professional game that was to eventually change his life. He made his league debut in November 1936 against Leeds as a wing-half and went on to make 23 appearances that season. He had just four outings the following campaign then retired from the game with injury problems. Instead he took up coaching and after the war was appointed manager of the England team. It was a position he held until 1963 when he was succeeded by Alf Ramsey.

WOMBWELL, RICHARD. Wombwell was already a well-travelled player when he came to United in 1905. He had begun his footballing career with Derby County in 1899 and had then played for Bristol City. Wombwell helped United to promotion in 1906 but then played only 14 games in the first division before signing for Hearts. He later returned to England to play with Brighton and Blackburn Rovers. He played 51 games for United, usually on the left wing.

WOOD, RAY. Busby Babe goalkeeper who survived the Munich air disaster. Wood was signed from Darlington in December 1949 and immediately stepped into the first team against Newcastle. But it was the only game he was to play for a number of seasons. It was not until late 1952 that he was to get a second chance but after that his appearances were more regular until he became first choice in the 1953–54 season. He won two championship medals with the club. He is probably best remembered, however, for the 1957 FA Cup final when he was injured following a collision with Aston Villa's Peter McParland. Wood's cheekbone was broken and he was stretchered off the field with Jackie Blanchflower forced to take over in the United goal. Wood returned later to play on the wing and then back in goal but he was a mere passenger, still dazed from the heavy collision. It was to be the pinnacle of Wood's United career. Less than a year later he crawled out of the wreckage of the crashed BEA Elizabethan Airliner at Munich and by the time he had recovered from his injuries, Harry Gregg had claimed the goalkeeper's jersey. Wood played just one more game for United and was then sold to Huddersfield Town in December 1958. He enjoyed a long career with Huddersfield before having spells with Bradford City and Barnsley. After that he took up an appointment as manager of Los Angeles and then as manager of the national Cyprus team. In all he had played just over 200 games for United.

WORLD CLUB CHAMPIONSHIP. United have competed in the World Club championship just once, qualifying after winning the European Cup in 1968. In September of that year they faced Estudiantes of Argentina, losing the first leg 0–1 in Buenos Aires. Unfortunately it was a game marred by brawling and the sending off of Nobby Stiles. The second leg, before 65,000, at Old Trafford was just as brutal an affair and ended in a 1–1 draw with a further two players sent off.

WORLD CUP FINALS. In 1966 Old Trafford was chosen as a venue for the World Cup finals. Three matches from group three were played at the ground involving Portugal, Hungary and Bulgaria.

WORST START. United hold the record for the worst ever start in the Football League when they lost every one of their first 12 games of the 1930–31 season. After 12 games they had won none, drawn none, lost twelve, scored 14 and conceded 49 goals. Not surprisingly they ended the season being relegated.

X. In football X traditionally stands for draw. The club record for the number of draws in a season was in 1980–81 when they drew 18 of their 42 fixtures.

XMAS DAY. There was a time when football was regularly played on Christmas Day but in recent years the footballing authorities have dropped the fixtures from their calendar. The last time United played on a Christmas Day was in 1957 when they beat Luton Town 3–0 at Old Trafford. Charlton, Edwards and Taylor scored the goals that day to send the United faithful back home full of Christmas cheer. Almost 40,000 turned up. The Christmas games, however, were not always so rewarding, especially during the 1930s when United dreaded that time of the year coming around. And usually it was Boxing Day when they took a hammering. On Boxing Day 1930 they lost 0–7 at Aston Villa and the following year went down by a similar score at Wolves. Then on Boxing Day 1933 Grimsby Town put another seven past United although they did manage three in reply.

Y

YOUNG PLAYER OF THE YEAR. The Professional
Footballers' Association award for Young Player of the Year
has been won by a United player on four occasions.
1985 Mark Hughes
1991 Lee Sharpe
1992 Ryan Giggs
1993 Ryan Giggs

YOUNGEST PLAYER. The youngest player to ever turn
out for Manchester United in a league match is Jeff
Whitefoot who made his league debut against Portsmouth
in April 1950. He was 16 years and 105 days old.

YOUTH. United first adopted a youth policy under manager
Matt Busby. Since then they have continued to place an
emphasis on discovering and nurturing young players. At
the forefront of this policy has been the club's participation
in the FA Youth Cup which they have won on a number of
occasions and which they held for five successive seasons
during the 1950s. Walter Crickmer and Jimmy Murphy
must also be given considerable credit for developing
United's youth policy during the 1950s. During the 1970s

and 80s, however, the youth policy was not maintained and only a few youngsters emerged to play first-team football. But the arrival of Alex Ferguson as manager brought a renewed emphasis on the scheme with young players like Lee Martin and Ryan Giggs soon bursting into the first team.

United have appeared in the FA Youth Cup final on nine occasions:

1952–53: 1st leg. Manchester United 7 Wolves 1; 2nd leg. Wolves 2 Manchester United 2. (Manchester United won 9–3 on aggregate.)

1953–54: 1st leg. Manchester United 4 Wolves 4; 2nd leg. Wolves 0 Manchester United 1. (Manchester United won 5–4 on aggregate.)

1954–55: 1st leg. Manchester United 4 West Brom 1; 2nd leg. West Brom 0 Manchester United 3. (Manchester United won 7–1 on aggregate.)

1955–56: 1st leg. Manchester United 3 Chesterfield 2; 2nd leg. Chesterfield 1 Manchester United 1. (Manchester United won 4–3 on aggregate.)

1956–57: 1st leg. West Ham United 2 Manchester United 3; 2nd leg. Manchester United 5 West Ham United 0. (Manchester United won 8–2 on aggregate.)

1963–64: 1st leg. Swindon Town 1 Manchester United 1; 2nd leg. Manchester United 4 Swindon 1. (Manchester United won 5–2 on aggregate.)

1981–82: 1st leg. Manchester United 2 Watford 3; 2nd leg. Watford 4 Manchester United 4 *aet.* (Watford won 7–6 on aggregate.)

1985–86: 1st leg. Manchester United 1 Manchester City 1; 2nd leg. Manchester City 2 Manchester United 0. (City won 3–1 on aggregate.)

1991–92: 1st leg. Crystal Palace 1 Manchester United 3; 2nd leg. Manchester United 3 Crystal Palace 2. (Manchester United won 6–3 on aggregate.)

1992–93: 1st leg. Manchester United 0 Leeds United 2; 2nd leg. Leeds United 2 Manchester United 1. (Leeds won 4–1 on aggregate.)

Z

ZENITH. United probably reached their zenith in 1968 when they became the first English club to win the European Cup. Had the Busby Babes not been so cruelly destroyed at Munich they would surely have added many more honours to the two league titles they had already claimed. The current United side must be rated as one of the finest in the club's history with four major trophies already in its collection and with players likely to add more.